MW00477472

*More Things in Heaven:*
*New and Selected Poems*

# MORE THINGS
# IN HEAVEN:
## NEW AND SELECTED POEMS

by

David Yezzi

Measure Press
Evansville, Indiana

The text of this book is composed in Baskerville.
Composition by R.G.
Manufacturing by Ingram.

Yezzi, David
  More Things in Heaven: New and Selected Poems / by David Yezzi — 1st ed.

  ISBN-13: 978-1-939574-33-6
  ISBN-10: 1-939574-33-1
  Library of Congress Control Number: 2022933084

Measure Press
526 S. Lincoln Park Dr.
Evansville, IN 47714
http://www.measurepress.com/measure/

Acknowledgments

The author is grateful to the editors of the following periodicals in which a number
of the new poems appeared:

*32 Poems*: "Sheep May Safely Graze"
*The Atlantic Monthly*: "Sugar on Snow"
*Bad Lilies*: "On a Street Piano," "Prepping the House," "Sirens for Sherod Santos"
*Birmingham Poetry Review*: "Ex Machina," "What's Changed"
*E-Verse Radio*: "The True Vine"
*Literary Imagination*: "More Things in Heaven"
*Literary Matters*: "One Hundred Umbrellas," "The Osprey," "Tyger, Tyger"
*Los Angeles Review of Books*: "Marina in Nervi"
*The New Criterion*: "Snowfall," "At the Station," "Death"
*Rosebud*: "The Spring"

"Sugar on Snow" appeared in *Poets of the Palisades* (The Poet's Press), edited by Paul
Nash, John Trause, et al.

"*The Flaying of Marsyas*" and "One Hundred Umbrellas" appeared in *The Eloquent
Poem: 128 Contemporary Poems and Their Making* (Persea), edited by Elise Paschen.

Thanks to the Bogliasco Foundation for its residency, during which a number of
these poems were written.

"Woman Holding a Fox," "Conversation of the Pharisees," "Hand to Mouth," "Sad
Is Eros, Builder of Cities," "Casco Passage," "Red Shift," "Oracle of the Great
Oak," "The Double." In *The Hidden Model* (2003). Copyright © 2003 by David Yezzi.
Published 2003 by TriQuarterly Books/Northwestern University Press. All rights
reserved.

"Mother Carey's Hen," "The Call," "The Good News," "Azores," "333 East 68th
Street," "Acceptance Speech," "Tritina for Susannah." In *Azores* (2008). Copyright
© 2008 by David Yezzi. This material is used by permission of Ohio University
Press, www.ohioswallow.com.

*for Sarah*

# CONTENTS

*x*

# Sugar on Snow

When you were young
you took me out
one night to where
you had been sugaring,

and we toasted
with our cups of snow
over which the amber
sweetness of trees

had been poured.
Each spring now I
check the taps, since
you have moved away.

Maybe it's the sleight
of hand of age, but each
year the sap sluices,
it seems, later and later,

too cold to run.
Another week, I tell myself.
If you have the secret,
it's there with you,

daughter. The woods
are poised to hear it,
and yet it will not come
and will not come.

# Ex Machina

*for Hal*

I've seen a god.
                    Seated on the patio,
a little drunk, I'm listening to Dylan, classic era,
on vinyl (mono), "Highway 61."
                              Geezer: I'm tired,
past the halfway, no longer hiding American Spirits
from the kids. So, it's twenty minutes
till we have to leave the house for a potluck
with some truly lovely, sweetly boring folks,
whose kids are friends with ours, the twins.
One boy texts to say he'll meet us there.
The other's on his way back from the park,
and I'm waiting for him — cold Negroni, music
blaring. I figure he'll be late as usual.

Then, in the lowlight of fall at six o'clock,
I look out on the street, over the wilted tree
(some species of deciduous something-
or-other), as he streaks by on his bicycle,
fast, fast, downhill, hair flying, Hermes,
a blur, a streak of white jersey, my son,
homing in the gloaming (and on time!). He's there,
then past. But I saw him: strapping, bold, coasting
in air, armored with teenage sweep and pride
against contingency and pain. Thank god,
thank god, I pray to him, may it be so.

# yger, Tyger

*They went to an abandoned home to smoke weed.*
*Inside, they found a tiger.*
— CNN

ong bud. Mind-splitting, hydroponic, pure indica body-high, one-hit weed,
own from Hawaiian seeds in a closet in a doublewide in Maine, up near Canada.

say it unleashed the tiger is to say everything and nothing. To say that they had
led to foresee the consequences of their actions is to be complicitly young.

e had the weed and Adam had the papers. And they'd been having sex, in fields
d organ lofts and in abandoned houses. Even so, you never forget your first tiger.

or had they dreamed it, like the Argentine writer Julio Cortázar, who imagined
w it might be possible to share a living space with a wild creature, or, more

the point how it would *not* be possible. What if the tiger claimed more and more
ace until the house was split in half? The parlors and the dining room

d the foyer and the stairs would become the tiger's, and the rest under threat,
amped and, because the thermostat was in the half gone out of bounds, cold.

here they were: the boy and the girl. And the weed, though they hadn't
en gotten around to smoking it, when this sleek shimmer and ripple

muscle entered the room. At first they were not afraid of it; rather they
lly expected that, wherever they went, extraordinary things would follow them,

d if that took the form of an emerald-eyed carnivore with a voice like a fault line,
en this was only different in degree and not in kind from what they had come

to feel was the new normal of their time together, both high and sober, either
in public, at the movies, under the Milky Way, in the bushes, or in the dark

secret confines of a house where no one had lived for years except a tiger.
There was nothing really strange about it, only that they began to fear for its

care over time: sweeping out the rooms, arranging for food and medicine
should the tiger fall ill with a viral infection or suppuration from an ingrown claw.

But wasn't it their tiger? They had found it. My tiger is your tiger, she had told him.
"Finding a forever home for a tiger is not easy," said the game warden, who took

the tiger in, bathed it and kept it in a cage, for future transfer to a willing zoo,
where its movements would be remarked on, the way that memories are,

at a distance, through wrought-iron bars, the tiger growing listless, eyes dimmed
except on those occasions when a pair of stoned kids, holding hands and pausing

before it, gaze in and recognize something familiar, and, full of mischief
and impunity, guided by a sense of natural law, whisper a secret plan to set it free.

4

# The Flaying of Marsyas

*for John Dubrow*

No one was much surprised when Marsyas
failed to outplay his rival on the aulos:
loud, upstart drunkard, fun until he's not.
They hung him upside down and set to stripping
away his skin — a grisly, painful death —
nailing it to a tree among the reeds,
the very ones his flute was fashioned from.

Two genial butchers carry out god's will,
as they construe it, paring back the fur
below the waist and down where fur turns flesh,
as a fellow satyr stands by with a bucket.
A faultless spaniel laps the pool of blood.
The question as to whether Marsyas
deserved a punishment this brutal seems
not to have troubled anyone till after,
and then as an unspoken, fleeting pang.

Amidst it all sits Titian (dressed as Midas),
his chin in hand, observing every stroke —
as we do here in this dim gallery —
pondering at an unbridgeable remove
the flyblown odor of the killing floor.
Eyes heavenward, the fiddler has left off playing,
as if, instead of melody, a question,
never said aloud but thought, ascends aloft
the way that prayers fly up, to wonder at
what misdeed made the god so very angry
he stopped the feral pipes of revelry.

# More Things in Heaven

When you have seen something, alone, just you,
you've got a choice: to keep it to yourself
or tell someone and keep on telling it
until they see it's true. Spoiler: they won't —
that's what you get for saying what you saw.
And, look, I'm not a fool. Can we be clear?
I didn't buy a word this guy was saying,
though *he* believed it — oh, hell yeah, he did —
the way he hung on every word just like
a birddog holds a pigeon, firm but living.
Dead pigeons, those we also got. Well, one.
I winged it with the blind man's BB gun.
(It's a mystery that I actually hit the thing!)
I'll get to that. But first: I meet the blind man.
His name is Carl, and, Carl, he was my landlord.
I had a bedroom upstairs in his house.
Carl was famous on the Avenue.
Everybody in the neighborhood
knew Carl, the tellers and the pizza guys.
Carl did Bikram yoga down the block,
and used a worn-out rope to walk his dog,
a collie he named Daisy — Daisy Dog.

The house, when I first got there, was a shambles —
a broken porch and yellowed paper shades
drawn down to the sills, which made it look
like maybe no one lived there. On the walk,
a metal front gate squealed and then fell off.

I sort of propped it up, since no one saw.
The thing I most remember when we met
was the fine translucent parchment of his lids
stretched tight across the hollows of his eyes.

I came around the corner of the house
and Carl was standing there holding his rifle.
He turned and sputtered out, "Hello? Who's there?"
He raised the gun and fired it in the rafters.
Three pigeons flew out from the timbered eaves.
"Damn rats with wings," Carl said, and turned to me,
"Where are you?" "Here," I said, and touched his arm.

The smoke had cleared out from the night before,
from cars first doused with gas then set on fire.

I lived a year with him. Some nights, I'd find
dog shit on the rug when I came home.
Carl just let it sit there for a week.
I'd hold my breath and scramble up the stairs
until the smell receded in the frozen air.
I had a cup. I had a radio that worked.
I had an ancient heater that glowed orange
as it grew hot. It pinged and groaned.
I had a chair, a desk, and a TV,
which didn't work, but that was fine. The smell
wore off after a minute or two, strange
what one gets used to — really anything.
From the windows I could see downtown
turn red and purple in the evening light.
Everything was far away and quiet.

Carl was smart, and he was also nuts.
I thought at first that he was paranoid.
His friend was off his meds, Carl liked to say —
a psycho, dangerous. He loved to tell it:
Tom was CIA, ex-CIA, he'd worked
for The Company, Carl said, and did I know
what that meant. I said, I did.
                                        Tom wore
a T-shirt and white painters pants. He helped
Carl around the place, repairing ironwork
and railings, missing floorboards, broken screens.
One day in fall, I found the two of them
talking on the porch. Carl was all excited
for me to meet Tom, and I shook his hand,
massive, callused, flecked in white house paint.
Tom was barrel-chested with thick arms
and wore thick black-rimmed glasses, like the ones
that poets used to wear after the war.
Carl's smiling, goading Tom to tell his story.
Tom just sits there looking at his feet,
a thousand miles away, snapping his gum.
So Carl can't help himself; he starts right in:
he tells me Tom was flown into Uganda,
on a diplomatic mission, him as muscle.
He was military, Tom was. "He knows how
to kill you with his bare hands," Carl says, laughing.
The airport's in Entebbe, Lake Victoria
the size of a whole country to the South:

"He gets there to the compound, and there's wire
and chain-link everywhere. They let them in,
and he starts walking down this path of fences.

They go into this courtyard, and then *BLAM!*,
Amin himself shoots Tom's friend in the head.
And then the lights go out. But they don't kill him;
they beat him up so bad that he can't walk.
When he wakes up, he's lying in the dirt,
but in a place he doesn't recognize.
Right, Tom?"

Tom says nothing, toeing a nail.

"They'd flown him to Kinshasa and left him there,
in an abandoned military post,
not a soul around to hear him call for help.
He crawls across the dirt, across the road,
toward a hut with a set of wooden stairs.
He can see brown rusted metal, he can see
barbed wire and the sky — blue, not a cloud.
He crawls until it's afternoon, then night.
His hands are tied. It hurts to stand. He reaches up
and turns a doorknob between his swollen hands.
The door is locked. He blacks out on the steps.
When Tom wakes up, a stewardess is asking
if he is comfortable and did he want
another blanket. He's lying in bed
on a plane back to Andrews, and she is there
to make sure he has everything he needs —
*everything*, if you know what I mean.
When he gets back to Langley, Jimmy Carter
arranges to meet him. Carter says sorry
for all that Tom has been through, and he says
that, if he wants to, he can kill Amin.
And when the time comes, Tom heads off to Jeddah,

and goes to visit Amin in the hospital,
where the Saudis were keeping him by then.
Amin was sleeping. He never woke up."
Carl got quiet then and shook his head
and smiled.

Tom looked at me without his eyes.

He was crying.

Sometimes I get a current in my fingers,
like an electric charge that's running through me.
It comes on me at night. I sit awake,
hunched in the darkness as it's pressing down.
When something dies, the part that slips away
is that cathodic charge beneath the skin.

Carl handed me the gun, when I first I met him,
with Daisy whimpering, bright-eyed, in a corner.
I fired in the rafters at the birds,
not even aiming. One flopped on the ground,
propped up on one wing, straining and then still.
Truth is, I lied. I did aim, best I could,
surprised at hitting what I'd actually meant to.
You think that you could never do a thing,
and then you do. I don't remember blood,
or barely, like a jewel. A voice got louder,
I handed back the gun.
Carl loaded it before we went inside.

Tom, I never saw but that one time.

# The True Vine

Pure cheese, I thought
when I was a kid. Dad loved
their stuff, life's blood — the lousy,
beery, stupid Irish Rovers.

Here in Baltimore, where
vinyl's cheap, I picked one up
for a buck, a Rover's record,
the whole group in green

polo necks; one's got on
an emerald bobble cap.
I almost chucked it today,
making space. It seemed lost

next to *Zeppelin III*, Kid
Ory, and the Diabellis,
like a tyro from RD-1 plunked down
in Port Authority. Instead,

I set the needle on it,
the songs still deeply hokey,
though there's tenderness, too,
as I listen now, or half-listen,

my mind flashing on a room,
where his fiercely guarded stereo
glowed, among glinting motes,
and where I'd hide out

while he was weeding in
the garden. His LPs
hissed and popped
from unlighted corners,

even this one in my hands,
its earworms boring home,
the doughty, toothy,
jangling Irish Rovers.

# Prepping the House

In quarantine, he took it on himself
to catch up with the odd jobs he'd been meaning
to get to if he only had the time. As it stood,
nothing had gotten done for many years
so that water leaked down from the upstairs baths
and paint-curls hung like gauzy spiders' nests
from the ceilings and the archways in the hall.
But now a guest was coming, and his pride
would not allow him to receive this stranger
in a house where the very walls and appliances
betrayed neglect. He would put things in order.

While his family napped or talked with friends remotely,
he set about repairing everything.
This pleased him. The work went well. He wasn't sure
what day his guest would come, and anyhow
it was more for himself, he told himself,
more for his peace of mind, amid the shutdowns;
the restaurants and the shops and schools were closed.

How long, he wondered, might the stranger linger?
Unclear. For now, he hoped his guest might feel
at home among his loved ones and his pets.
As for his needs, who knew? Though he imagined
they could be quite elaborate, his stay
proprietary and indefinite.

# What's Changed

The thing that stung me most after you died
was how I couldn't tell my news to you.
It made it so my good days barely mattered.

Nearer your age today, I realize
surprisingly — because it's unfamiliar —
that just now I am ludicrously happy.

I think of you, how pleased you were to hear
when things were going well, when life was all
you'd hoped for me, your daily, inward prayer.

I feel you here. A house wren chirps outside.
An airplane rides home in the higher air.
So quiet you can hear me — leaves, a breeze.

An hour on, this windfall will be gone.
This news is for you alone. I say it quickly,
while I am once again, briefly, your son.

# he Spring

I've come back      with a wife and children    to this volcanic coast,

views and bays.      The islanders believe      these minerals heal the body,

calm the mind.      *Salute per aqua.*    From small jars we scoop

ooth, olive mud,      which the man below      the stairs prepares.

The mud's dark green      and dries to gray.      When it has drawn

oils from our skin      and left its talc of minerals,      we wash off its cumuli

in sea water.    Does it work?    Yes, of course,    we think, under the clouds,

awn like drapes      on a blinding sky.    And yet there's something

that water cannot wash away.    A thousand years has not altered    this rock.

e sea burns and cools.    We've come a hard way      to these curing waters.

# On a Street Piano

Outside the library
of this seaside town
each summer an old
upright is set out —

wildly painted, its
row of teeth, tarred
and yellow. It's here
for anyone who

wants it: *Anytime*
says the rain-proof sign.
I have a tune I like to try;
others have theirs.

Songs slip through
an open window, past
the giveaway pile,
the bug-eyed tamtam from

Vanuatu, three pewter
pitchers, and a curling chart
of Jericho Bay.
Now a child — is it? —

plays at scales.
Someone's hands, not
mine, could charm
a summer night with it.

My sons, of course,
are horrified, at their
age. At mine, I'm more
inured to shame.

The young librarian
smiles as I pass her.
She knows me
by my broken song.

# Sheep May Safely Graze

In darkness, with the smell of tallow hanging
in the damp around his desk, he dips his pen
to scratch another melody across
the topmost staff, the left hand speaking back
to the right then flying up, a finch above
the keyboard he has pictured in his mind.

The church is cold where yesterday he laid
to rest the second of his twins, a girl,
Maria Sophia, outlasting her brother
by only a few weeks. Johann Christoph
survived just long enough to have a name
and his father's love. He went the day he came.

Alone in Weimar, with Goethe not yet born,
and the scythe of history sleeping in the wheat,
he listened to the notes that made no sound,
giving himself completely to the laws
of counterpoint alive in every key,
and, ruled by them, composed a song of praise.

# French Suites

i. One Hundred Umbrellas

*Arcueil, 1916*

After so long, I've finally arrived
exactly . . . . where? Well, *here*. Yes, here, for sure:
a lampless street, an obscure neighborhood,
outside the walls, an hour's walk from town.
I gave up town. Now what do I have left?
A tiny dolor I've fed on for decades —
this pang is now the full scope of my gift.
But thankfully that's nothing at all to you.
I'm so glad you're here. You're good to come.
I've been turned down before, yes, many times,
by women who could clearly use the money,
artists' models mostly, like she was.
That dress you're trying on should fit you well.
It's stolen from the Ballet Russe, a getup
that Bakst designed for *Boris Godunov*.
I took it last night from the costume shop.
It's possible I'd had a bit to drink.
Did I tell you that I'm writing ballets now?
Me and Picasso. Yes, and Jean Cocteau,
that imbecile. So earnest and effete.
Pablo's more my taste. He's *dee*-vious.
And yet his sets — of cardboard! — Cubist, so . . .
well, striking in a nonsense sort of way.
His kind of nonsense, though, makes too much sense.

Perhaps you'll come one night. We'll go together.
 And, please don't worry,
with that screen between us, you can be discreet.
It's Japanese. Do you admire the work?
Indoors, it's cherry blossoms; outside, it's snow!
And freezing rain, then, finally, merely rain.

Rain.

 Sleet.

 Rain.


Gray water threads the jet-black paving stones
in rivulets around the egg-shaped cobbles,
then back together and apart again,
before joining with the torrent in the gutters,
churning downhill like springtime in a valley.
Have you been to the South? One day you will,
when you are older. You will love the Alps.
You think I'm joking, but I never joke.
I sometimes smile, though that's by accident.
Occasionally, back when she was there —
the one I mentioned, Suzanne Valadon —
a smile would cross my face like a spooked bird
for a second and then vanish, registered
only by her surprise, a passing shade.
The things I say must seem quite strange to you,
but I am not a madman, nor this a hoax.
It's just the way I am, a little . . . *what?*
It's true: I only like to eat white foods:
eggs, sugar, shredded bones, and certain fish

without their skins; fat from dead animals,
chicken cooked in water, moldy fruit,
rice, turnips, sausages in camphor, veal,
salt, coconuts, white cheeses, cotton salad.
I boil my wine and drink it mixed with fuchsia.
I love to eat, although I never talk
at mealtimes, lest I suffocate myself.
*I breathe with care, a little at a time*:
all that she knew.

Sleet's ticking at the windows. Sleet and ice
are not my elements. I like the rain.
It rains in Paris in the key of D.

You see this painting? I was younger then.
My hair is long in back and I affected
a stovepipe hat. I think that was the happiest
I've ever been. Spring 1893.
You see how foolish she has made me look.
Biqui, I called her. *Bonjour, Biqui, Bonjour.*
She painted it when we two lived together.
In separate flats. And I would play for her
a song to say good morning through the wall.

The rain has made a lake of dirty water.
There's black and then there is blacker than black.
There's nothing mystical about what vexes me,
but, at night, I play it over in my mind
eight hundred times (but first, an hour of quiet).

I'm boring you. Please, will you have a drink?
I think I will, if you don't mind. Absinthe

is just *anise* plus poison. Light through fog
calls home the small boats from the storm-tossed sea.

                             I know this place
is not so tidy. I had to fire the maid.
She made me itch, a very haughty person,
very arrogant. I always felt her eyes.
But you don't judge me, do you? No, my dear.
You are an angel, heaven's purest creature.
I'm not a slob; I just can't part with things —
magazines, newspapers. I've kept a record . . .
Here's April 13, 1893,
the last night that we spent with one another.
We'd been to see the show at the Grande Palais.
She jumped out the window when she left me.
No one will think of me when I am gone.

You're wondering at these umbrellas, my dear?
I admit they look quite frightening at night.
I find them on my trips into the City.
Sad creatures, wind-wracked birds with broken pinions
lying in gutters or crashed onto the quay,
or under porticoes in the Marais.
A few still work. This one is cut bamboo.
Its slender bones expand to lift its wings
against the midday sun or cold spring rain,
like the one we have tonight that won't let up.
After, you'll take it as a souvenir.
I miss the City, but way leads on to way.
These wounded dinosaurs are my mementoes,
like a tune of 18 bars ad infinitum,
because extinction sounds like that,

played over just the same each time, forever.

I walked to town today. I like to walk.
And now I have a blister on my toe.
I saw no one and yet it felt like home.
The markets of Montparnasse, the sculpted gardens,
the people to-ing and fro-ing on the stones,
a tussle overflowing the café.
Ha! Such wildness. Here, we have the rain,
a drip, a drop, a hovering mist of gray.
I worry that we'll meet around a corner.
I see her dressed in black outside the church;
I see her disappearing down an ally;
I see her in a taxi going by,
behind the high glass of an atelier,
nude, posing for her lover, or she's painting
in the sun of Montmartre in the afternoon,
in that same square that she knew as a girl,
growing up without a father, in the streets.

The umbrella is a devilish machine,
as if flown from the blind recess of history
to die in a heap on the Pont Neuf. Or sometimes:
I steal them out of cloak rooms when the staff
are smoking cigarettes or hailing taxis.
I can't resist my lust for gorgeous things.
Look: this one has a mallard's head. How fitting,
a duck in a downpour, beads on its back.
The streets tonight are filled with mercury.

Here's to you.
You see the fairy dancing in the flame

in green chiffon, like one of Degas's dancers?
Absinthe is a green fairy, so they say.
She's cold and growing smaller every year.
I hate her. I adore her. Her white skin
is the latest inspiration of Degas.
She often takes her clothes off for him now.

When you are dressed and ready, you may
behave as cruelly as you like, the crueler,
the better. Though, in truth, she wasn't cruel,
not wantonly. She didn't mean to be
uncaring toward me, though she never loved me.
That much I know, and when she realized
that it was so, she never came again.
She left a shelf of things: perfume, a brooch,
a snake with ruby eyes — a gift no doubt —
this portrait of me, and this satin dress.
I confess it is no costume. It was hers.
The one you're wearing now. Come, let me see you.
One minute while I take away the screen.

*O worthless fool: she left no dress, there's no one . . .*
*No, that's not it. I am not mad.    She's here:*

                                        So beautiful.
Perhaps you'll come again tomorrow night?

Or stay a while, at least until it stops,
the rain. *Shh.* Listen, like a tune. You'll stay.

              Rain.           Rain.

Rain.

## ii. Marina in Nervi

*Paris 1926*

My father called that place our paradise:
that was its name, the Golfo Paradiso —
with olive trees, high cactuses and palms,
quince trees in December, bougainvillea
gone riot on the schist along the coast,
orange-glow pyracantha, butcher's-broom,
and sunlight in the morning on the mountains.
I couldn't wait to leave it. Why was that?
Today, it seems a precious memory.
My sin was squandering. And now I'm being
punished for my sin. I've been cast out.

O little girl, my one light, my Irina,
what did I do to you? How very cold
you must have been. It hurts to think of it —
so hungry all the time, so very hungry,
the pain of it eating daily at your limbs,
your thought when you woke up, your midnight thought
that barely let you sleep. Your body ached
until there was not food enough to stoke
the tiny flutter of your heart or fill
your lungs. I thought the orphanage would feed you,
but you died on a cot in a freezing corridor.
*Io non piangëa, sì dentro impetrai.*
And then we starved, and Moscow was our prison.

For two nights I have dreamt about the sea,
the *pensione* below the Apennines,

the switchback paths that took us to the beach.
I was a girl, like you, though I was older.
The hotelier's son was my age and so quiet.
I never spoke to him, but we would catch
each other's eyes whenever he was working
in the garden where we children took our breakfast
or on the pavements overgrown with succulents.
His talent was for painting. He had learned
the trompe-l'oeil style they practice in that region.
From my window I would watch him on a scaffold
restoring faded stucco cornices,
faux curtains blowing out of open shutters,
all make believe, ascribing depth to flatness
with his brush. That summer, I believe, I loved him,
just puppy love — though still I think of him.
He painted with considerable skill,
no writer, thank god. I loved him more for that.
Heaven has room for gifted artisans,
but poets, for their sins, are rarely saved.
So much the better, Mother liked to say.

Poor Mother was the reason we had gone
to winter in Liguria. Her health was bad.
Her doctor recommended a milder climate,
clear air and sun. Then, Nervi was a spa,
with villas in the overhanging hills
and the passeggiata like a beached leviathan,
where I would wheel out her rattan recliner,
with blankets heaped up on her lap and scarves
around her neck and set her in the sun.
Tucked in against the cliff-face, she would sit
for hours with the villagers and tourists,

basking in the hothouse of low light
and counting as the little fishing boats
went out and came back past the rocky breakwater.
And dogs on leashes leapt to meet their friends,
whose owners brought them each day without fail,
so that we learned their names — Allegro, Jacquie.
In her flowing layers underneath the palms
she looked like a grande dame out of Matisse,
and for a while we could forget her illness,
though her pale face always told a different story.

And when the winds came unexpectedly
that autumn, we all kept inside. I heard
the constant rattle of the great French doors
that opened on my bedroom balcony
rumble and thud as if the wind had made
them angry to be bolted shut all day.
And through the shaking glass I watched with awe
the giant palm tree bend as if to break
and in a lull come to itself again
until, frightened by its violent back and forth,
I had to look away. Then came the rain.
I remember in Camogli how the surf
churned up the beach of polished, palm-sized stones
each time it drew back, and the sound it made
was of bed linens slowly torn for bandages
by nurses who are caring for the wounded.
But then after a week or so the sun
would find me out where I had squirreled away
and lure me out of doors in the dying breeze
and up the chalky cliffside, clambering.
On clear days, when the sun shone on the sea

like the momentary blinding of a flashbulb,
I felt happy. The grand houses and hills
seemed new-born, as if scrubbed clean of their demons.

But you can't eat the landscape, nor can memories
of pleasant days sustain you longer than
a sudden reverie in which the book
you're holding drops beside your chair, the pages
splaying out like a vision of the sea
as it occludes your pain with its narcotic.
Worn off again, those thoughts come crashing back,
incessant waves, the rush and cry of spume,
threading through the rocks and surging up
in plumes of spray, then falling back again
into the vast, engulfing, unopposable ocean.

These days we rarely see the sun,
your sister and I. And the cleansing light,
which made me feel the world had been redeemed,
here serves merely to shine a light on Hell,
its recesses and obscure depths, which delve
more deeply than I ever knew was possible.
We ate the horses.

In dreams these past two nights, I saw myself
walking the passeggiata with my eyes
cast down, combing the paving stones to find
a button that had fallen from my dress,
close to my heart. It must have popped off when
I was chasing after Jacquie and Allegro.
How foolish I was to wear my new clothes
to play with dogs. I hoped the owner's boy —

what was his *name?* — might like to see me in them.
I never think of dresses now, but that
sea-blue one was my favorite possession.
And stupidly I ruined everything.
I seethed and cursed myself, and I cursed God
for taking from me what I loved the best.
The secrets of my future happiness
were layered in those whorls of nacreous
pearl, my fingers fumbling with them each morning,
as I looked out over the charcoal inlet.
Vanished. Lost. Gone for good — an odd expression.
Then after an hour of walking and hot tears —
crying, cursing, stomping back and forth —
I found it glinting in a patch of sunlight,
as if that single shaft had guided me
to it, my good thing, mine again, returned.
That day I could believe in answered prayers.
Our nanny teased me, sewing it back on,
and by dinner it was as if I'd never lost it.

*O idiot, you hopeless idiot.*

It's funny I should think about that now.
It seems as if it happened to a stranger.
How far away that coast is and that girl.
You hear the church bell? Is it there or here,
clanging the hour in Saint-Sulpice? It's hot.
The caged electric fan mimics the slow,
incessant churning of water on the rocks.
That day the tempest overturned the lampposts,
and piled the little harbor with debris.
The villagers came out, as after a shipwreck,

smiling amazedly at the rough water,
grateful for the sunlight peeking through
the fuchsia clouds above the quieting sea.
I wish that you had been there, my Irina.
Surely, I'll never see that place again.

# Sirens for Sherod Santos

Thanks, poet, for the rainy poem I read
the year I learned of love and the pain of love.
I found your book in a bookstall in a white-florescent
mall, when I was a student and all poets were dead.

You wrote about bad weather in autumn and of sirens
echoing like mating calls down the glistening streets.
Sirens implied a warning, I knew — someone was sick
or in distress, a kitchen fire had leapt out of control.

But they were far away, their urgency swallowed
by the sound of downspouts trickling into gutters.
O blessèd time, when all that the heart enacted
still seemed in beautiful fulfillment of the world.

Today, sirens are nearer. We hear them, one and then
another, in all kinds of weather, high winds and sun.
They whine through screens, and their alarum is general,
though each one — hear it? — exhales its own shrill cry.

# Snowfall

A light snow falls through an ashy sky.
From the city no sounds rise up, no human cries,

not the grocer's call or the ruckus of his cart,
no light-hearted song of being young and in love.

From the tower in the piazza, the quinsied hours
moan, sighing as if from a world far off.

Flocks of birds beat against the misted glass:
ghosts of friends returned, peering in, calling to me.

Soon, O my dears, soon — peace, indomitable heart —
I will sift down to silence, in shadow rest.

(GIOSUÈ CARDUCCI)

# At the Station

*In an autumn morning*

O the lamps — how they chase
each other lazily there behind the trees,
yawning their light through dripping
branches onto the mud.

Faint, fine, shrill, a nearby
steam engine hisses. A lead sky
and the autumn morning
enwrap us like a great chimera.

Where and to what are they going, these people,
cloaked and silent, hurrying to dark cars —
to what unforeseeable sorrows
or pangs of remote hope?

Even you, rapt Lydia, give
to the conductor your torn ticket,
and to pressing time your beautiful years,
your memories and moments of joy.

Along the black train come
the trainmen hooded in black
like shadows, with dim lanterns
and iron sledges, and the iron

brakes when plied make a long
enervated clang: from the soul's depths,
an echo of languor makes its sad
reply, like a shudder.

And the doors slammed shut
seem like outrages: a quick jibe
sounds the final farewell:
thundering on heavy panes, the rain.

Already the monster, owning its metallic
soul, fumes, slouches, pants, opens
wide its fiery eyes; defies the heavens,
whistling through the gloom.

The unholy monster goes; with a horrible tug,
beating its wings, it carries away my love.
Ah, the alabaster face and fine veil,
hailing me, disappear in darkness.

O sweet face of pale rose,
o starlit placid eyes, o snow-white
forehead ringed with luxuriant curls
gently bending in a nod of love.

The warm air was throbbing with life;
the summer throbbed when she looked on me,
and the youthful June sun
liked to shower her cheek

with kisses of light, reflected through
auburn hair: like a halo
more brilliant than the sun, my dreams
encircle her soft shape . . .

Beneath the rain, I return through
the haze; and I would lose myself in it.
I stagger like a drunk. I touch myself
to see if I also have become a ghost.

O how the leaves are falling — cold,
incessant, mute, heavy — on my soul.
I know that everywhere in the world,
solitary and eternal, it is November.

Better he who's lost the sense of life,
better this shadow, this haze:
I want O how I want to lie myself down
in doldrums that will last forever.


(GIOSUÈ CARDUCCI)

# Death

*During a diphtheria epidemic*

When the precise diva drops down on our houses,
the far-off roar of her flying is heard,

and the shadow of her icy wing, icily advancing,
spreads wide a sad silence.

When she comes, men bow their heads,
but the women fall to pining.

Thus the treetops, when July winds gather,
do not sway on the green hills:

the trees stand almost utterly still,
and only the hoarse moan of the creek is heard.

She enters, passes, touches, and without even turning levels
the saplings, delighted by their young branches;

she shears the golden wheat, and strips even hanging grapes,
scoops up the good wives and innocent girls

and tiny children: pink between black wings they reach their arms
to the sun, to their games, and smile.

O sad homes, where before their fathers' faces,
silent, livid diva, you put out young lives.

Therein, rooms no longer sound with laughter and merrymaking
or with whispers, like birds' nests in May:

therein, no more the sound of joyful rearing,
nor love's woes, nor wedding dances:

they grow old therein, the shadowed survivors; to the roar
of your return their ears incline, O goddess.

*June 27, 1875*

(GIOSUÈ CARDUCCI)

# The Osprey

High water sucked the beach clean of debris.
High winds downed boughs and the high osprey's nest.
She perches on a driftwood log, half-dead,
eyes on the tide, without her fledglings now.

All June she dropped fish in the crowded aerie,
its crown of twigs topping a patchy pine:
the racket then, like bagpipes on the sea
blown by a piper still drunk in the morning.

We wondered if without her nest she'd go.
She was our bird, her cry our intimate,
a siren-wail each time we crossed the beach.
*Rebuild*, poor mama bird, we thought. But no.

Nor has she left completely, her hard drone
continuing, though not to do with us,
an obbligato rifling the wind,
a radar beacon that sends back no ping.

We see her at the tops of farther trees,
without a place to shelter, keeping watch
over the broken nest, the blasted pine,
scanning the rocks for something left to guard.

*from* The Hidden Model *(2003)*

# Woman Holding a Fox

Buried inside, page 3, below the fold,
a woman crumpled on fresh dirt begins to get the gist:
that she has lost the use of her left leg, that when she tripped
        her hip gave out. Shock explains
this all to her, a self-assured young doctor mouthing, *Rest*.

The reason for the break, a rabid fox
that came at her when she stepped out for half a cigarette.
Age seventy-nine, the paper said; she hadn't toppled far,
        merely down her few front steps,
but late enough that no one finds her till the following day.

And here's the eerie part. Just when she thinks
to drag herself down to the curb, the twisted fox comes back.
In hours her arms are bitten blue, waving her one defense.
        Her glasses lost in tufted grass,
she hears it thread the underbrush before she sees it leap.

At 2 o'clock, a nurse toggles the lamp.
Something for the pain. Since after dark, the fox has come
to look on her as prey, the way he circles then descends.
        This is no dream, she tells herself.
Yet it had seemed unreal from the initial streak of red:

a comedy at first, a photo-op,
then something else, an eye-white flash our unsuspecting trust
shields us from until the outward show no longer jibes.
        She's landed in her garden row,
her Marlboro still smoking on the carefully weeded path.

Beyond the gate a sunset has begun,
the swatch of sky above her roof dyed jacaranda-blue.
These are things she sees as she assumes things can't get worse.
But then they do. When it returns,
she clasps it to herself. Somehow she's managed to affix

small hands around its muzzle and bared teeth.
All night she feels it panting and enraged, then weirdly calm.
So off and on for hours until someone spots her there.
A neighbor comes, she knows that now.
But on the sedge she hadn't guessed that it would end so well.

As for what crowds her head: a single thought
repeated in contrition, while the same minute extends,
infinitely regressing between mirrors set opposed.
Music's playing down the hall,
carried on a crack of light that shows the door ajar.

It's nearly dawn. I have not killed the fox,
my arms barely keep him hemmed, my fingers have gone limp.
Across the lawn an amniotic slick of dew gives off
a silver sheen and sudden cold.
I'm glad you happened by, she wryly croaks when he appears.

Before he batters in the hissing fox,
he asks her why she simply didn't let it run away.
I know this creature pretty well by now. She shows her skin.
It's true, she understands the fox
and wonders if she hasn't always known that he was there,

known it when her first child was born,
and known it, too, the day her husband died three years ago.
At any rate she knows it now, will always keep him close
in her embrace from day to day,
up to a time when memories of these no longer serve.

# Conversation of the Pharisees

*after Rembrandt's "Hundred Guilder Print"*

Such upright citizens, all honest Joes,
    these legal men sketched in at left
so sparingly they almost blanch from view;
        how they huddle,
    dull to radiance

and fouled in the lines affixing them,
    oblivious to Christ's light caught
across their faces, like a harrowing
        of their tight circle,
    as they natter on.

A few, you say, acknowledge Him and turn
    intently or with skepticism
intact — still, they have understood more than
        their purblind fellows,
    who, while arguing

arcana of scripture with which to test
    the man, have left off noticing
what even children and the sick see plainly.
        And we are quick
    to read the gulf between

ourselves and those gray priests in antique hats
    (aligned instead with the heroes),
and wise to the fact of their ignorance,
        though we, like them,
    have missed the central point:

that they are there for us, to represent
        those from whom the truth's been held,
the more bemused, who lord the blameless life,
        its sureties,
     over the fallen ones.

We, too, have mastered certainties, taken solace
       in precision, keeping dates,
and the long code of standard practices
       like compositions
    bitten into brass,

while laws we've missed, or lapsed in looking for,
       remain of necessity
unremarkable and always close,
       so many motes
    adrift in dark corners.

# Hand to Mouth

"How much is enough?" she snorted, gamely
twisting a sprig of watercress in the air
then straining its jade leaves through her bright teeth,
and I thought of some friends we knew in Brooklyn —
he a painter, she a perfect four
who made her money as a mannequin,
a fit-model on 7ᵗʰ Avenue.
Childless, they kept a German Shepherd bitch
who managed better on beef bones and lettuce
than they on what they ate most days. Each week,
they'd lug another sack of kibble home,
and for themselves brown rice in five-pound bags.

The dog died; they survived, as it turned out.
(He wolfed a ball of cord that gave his guts
a snarl the hospital despaired of cutting.
Hand-tied, they put him down.) Last we heard,
the two had gone to Greece and thrown themselves
upon the kindness of an island village,
where he became a goatherd, work that paid
for food enough. For shelter, they relied
on balmy weather, lean-tos, and cleared ground.
No recent news has made it back, except
that they've become a nuisance in the town.
And though the snow's arrived there, they're still gone.

So we lose touch, like with the newlyweds,
who sold our wedding gifts and moved out West.

We hadn't missed them much, till common friends
reported recently the two have split.
He's lost his mind again (believes he's Christ)
and disappeared more fully than the friends
we keep as enemies, whom we still prize,
since secretly we can't abide a world
that they're not in, so rather than expel
them fully from our thoughts we hold them close
and scorn them, as they do us, with the same
shared venom, although once we called it love.

How different are the friendships that endure:
inviolate, well-founded, decorous,
though never seared by that eruptive heat
that harms the people closest to our hearts.
And so we keep the things we never had.
The blithe acquaintances we hardly mind —
those who take our calls, or meet for lunch,
commiserate (we'd do the same for them) —
have let us know that, while we are not loved,
we are well-liked. Just so, the opposite:
it's those we have that we will surely lose,
those focal points that show the world slip by.

Across the oaken restaurant, a woman
has reddened into tears, and we're at pains
to know if she's just broken with the guy
who slides his chair and walks to comfort her.
A stiff embrace broadcasts their rapprochement
to other furtive onlookers like us
who trust that they have made it up for now,
although their rift might open up the same

tomorrow night, or some night in the span
allotted them from their communal time
in this city and while they both are young
and getting by (or not) on God knows what.

# "Sad Is Eros,
# Builder of Cities"

*A wrecking site, Lower East Side*

Leveled to a ruin of cinder block,
the walls and gimcrack shards of tenement
make a more enduring bid for order:

No further demolition will undo
this present lack, no bright ascendancy
seduce its will or struggle to climb back.

It marks a certain beauty, a blank snow
hugging the swaddled torso of the ground
in mended white, a uniform, a gown.

Draped piecemeal in a length of bridal cloth,
the sky meets its reflection, tinted dun
with the pallor of this lacuna's crumbled stone.

Perhaps the planners have already drawn
fresh blueprints for another building here,
yet something of the place itself resists

such strivers' fragile meddling and scolds
the futility of each attempt torn down —
if no time soon, still, some day: Do not build.

# Casco Passage

*In mem. Paul Wood, d. 1999*

By midday, gouts of fog
          sock in until
we almost think the weather means some harm,
the way it runs over the harbor. Gauzy,
          a trawler on its mooring
          sputters close to home.
                    A level calm.
Seams smoothed, the clouded archway shadowless:
our view lacks eye-holds, like the papered set
          of a photo shoot, merely
                    figure and ground.

          This morning, as we slept,
                    his boat was found
grinding in circles somewhere up the reach.
A fisherman came on it stymied there,
          recrossing in the spume
          of its own wake, its wheelhouse
                    ghostly, its course
a ring by Titian charcoaled in the sea.
We knew his name. And when it made the news
          the dust of pickups rose
                    to clog the road:

          men set out dragging rigs
                    that yesterday
had yanked up heavy, bruised with mussel shells,
Phoenician purples clustered in a fist.

Today, they're hoisted limp —
a heartache and relief.
           One snarled clue:
some fouled line sliced from the sinking trap.
Had it jerked him in a whip-crack overboard,
           his strength sapped as he flailed
                to loose his boat?


           Now shoals of mackerel lash
                in running shallows,
each silver leap skyward through glass survived.
Down on the point, a few last headlights glare,
           then swing wide, then go.
           I have come to the water
                to clean a pail,
while you close out the damp in half-lit rooms.
A year ago, we married near this spot,
           where three white pine trees stare
                over the bay.


           All week, his wife can watch
                hope's half-life split
daily until the hour she knows he's gone.
But for now: she looks on as he swims
           ashore — "he's strong, you know?" —
           chokes breath on sand . . . *No sign.*
                Word goes round,
as stories of near-misses start in town:
"Remember in the south, that killing gale?
           After the second night,
                with the helm

*51*

an icy sledgehammer
whanging my ribs,
I leaned down to your mother, who for days
could not look at the waves as high as roofs.
'We'll die out here,' I told her,
letting the tiller go;
'I'm so damn tired . . .'
The wind was through with us two hours later.
Half-sunk, we made land under perfect skies,
boys out hauling nets
struck by the sun."

# Red Shift

What had seemed till recently as clear as day
darkens now, beaten to violet breakers,

whose troughs' deep indigos amaze all hands,
befogging, separatist as ampersands

or the dotted line land divides along.
No bearings in this blue, no channel gong

to hark us back from our wrong turn, no scenes
of harbor, of islands wood-smoked and greening.

Still, in light of all that we've remarked
of sudden weather and the yellow stars,

best to batten down, stand watch for signs
of orange at evening, or a slackening in the lines,

trusting that this time of red alert might ease
its frequency, back in pacific seas.

# Oracle of the Great Oak

Forget your question a while.
                              First, turn and see
the roadway threading squares of winter wheat,
fences bound with scrub. Take in the town,
its rooftops like masterstrokes of royal blue.
And notice, too, the crazed geometry
of broken cornstalks bristling the hills,
how balanced perfectly beneath a wisp
of cumulus they jut in freezing gray.
This equipoise comes rarely, as you know.
I don't say *never*. I myself have felt
such calm before, though seldom:
                              As a child,
I woke in sunlight on my parents' berth
aboard a packet moored in a fjord.
The hush beneath its glowering cliffs spread out
like palms laid on an altar, and the sea
along the Norwegian coast, as cold as death,
shone dazzling, benign. That was the first.
Then later at the university
of Freiburg, as a young man I heard bells
at a garret window mix with water-sound
careering through the streets in ancient troths.
The markets smelled of coffee and spilt beer.
Strange what one remembers, stranger still
to think how these oases of rapt thought
could lead one here.
                              How have I come this way?

I hardly know. Nor can I tell you why
I chose to stay, or how then I became
the voice of this arthritic tree, though not
its saying's source. It couldn't matter less.
My gift is, well, hardly a gift at all,
like speaking different languages from birth.
I've learned that I am home, that I'll be buried
beside this fist of roots. Not long from now.
In the meantime, travelers find their way to me,
each harboring his query for these boughs.

With gifts and food they leave, I have enough.
Who would disturb this peace?
                            Our end is known.
This great oak speaks through me, the tranced-out ape
of its thoughts, the medium, if you will, through which
the sound of leaves coheres in speech. The rest:
a rustling resolved into, not reason,
but darker figures suited to our fates.
There's the message, there's the tree, and there is I.
Mostly, the branches thrash like metal grates,
a shivaree to toast the marriage bed
grinding down to groans of factories,
or a rustling of innumerable books —
their pages safe from Alexandrian fires
or the dozing aesthete's fumbled cigarette —
conveying their immortal, hidden will
that no one, not the god himself, controls.
I've seen the faithful crumble with the weight
of knowing what befalls our brittle lives.
You're having second thoughts?
                            Well. It is late.

In truth, it's better not to ask, I've found;
the news is never good, and it infects
the seeker with a plague that courses through him
until he's pure contagion. Yet they come,
and leave much as you will, though blinder than
when they arrived. A sickness eats their eyes.
Below, you'll find a hotel on the square.
Just say you met me here; no need for names.
Tell them you climbed the hill and that we spoke,
that in the morning you will start for home.
Goodnight. How fortunate: you see the moon
that leads you on the path and me to bed?

# The Double

On Sheep Meadow an old man picks his way
past sunning bodies, which, though its early April,
fill the grass. The wind lifts up his coattails,
flings them sidelong, flapping against his cane
       in the distance.

And as he comes across the wide expanse
of green he seems to float over blowing shoals,
walking on the risen Styx, and hunched,
for old men tire easily (he is tired)
       on windy passages.

But wind has power to blur the wobbly world:
a tall man certainly, but hardly old —
my age, in fact. How had there been a cane?
Unless the brain works with the eye to fill in
       for gaps we find.

Now close, he looks like me. Strange to think
that he's no nearer age and death than I,
the young man walking out of the older man
like a snake skin shed, the same one he will wear
       again someday.

*from* Azores *(2008)*

# Mother Carey's Hen

There are days I don't think about the sea;
        weeks wash by in fact,
then a shearwater — or some such — flutters by
on the salt flats fanning out in my mind's-eye,
reflected there, a shimmering reverie,
            recalling the pact

I once made (and renew today) to hold
        to a higher altitude.
But note the difference between this bird
and me: a slight disruption or harsh word
and I crash, folded seaward, letting cold
           life intrude;

whereas the petrel, mindless of such height,
        scales each watery hill
that rises up, adapting to the shape
of each impediment, each low escape
instinct in it, the scope of its flight
           fitted to its will.

# The Call

The call comes and you're out. When you retrieve
the message and return the call, you learn
that someone you knew distantly has died.
His bereaved partner takes you through the news.

She wants to tell you personally how
he fought and, then, how suddenly he went.
She's stunned, and you feel horrible for her,
though somewhat dazed, since he was not a friend,

just someone you saw once or twice a year,
and who, in truth, always produced a shudder:
you confess that you never liked him much,
not to her, of course, but silently to yourself.

You feel ashamed, or rather think the word
*ashamed*, and hurry off the line. That's when
the image of him appears more vividly,
with nicotine-stained fingertips and hair

like desert weeds fetched up on chicken wire,
the rapacious way he always buttonholed
you at a launch, his breath blowsy with wine.
Well, that will never ever happen again:

one less acquaintance who stops to say hello,
apparently happy at the sight of you.
So why then this surprising queasiness,
not of repulsion but of something like remorse

that comes on you without your guessing it,
till the thing that nagged you most – his laugh, perhaps –
becomes the very music that you miss,
or think you do, or want to, now he's gone.

# The Good News

A friend calls, so I ask him to stop by.
We sip old Scotch, the good stuff, order in,
some Indian — no frills too fine for him
or me, particularly since it's been
           ages since we made the time.

Two drinks in, we've caught up on our plans.
I've sleepwalked through the last few years by rote;
he's had a nasty rough patch, quote-unquote,
on the home front. So, we commiserate,
           cupping our lowballs in our hands.

It's great to see him, good to have a friend
who feels the same as you about his lot —
that, while some grass is greener, your small plot
is crudely arable, and though you're not
           so young, it's still not quite the end.

As if remembering then, he spills his news.
Though I was pretty lit, I swear it's true,
it was as if a gold glow filled the room
and shone on him, a sun-shaft piercing through
           dense clouds, behind which swept long views.

In that rich light, he looked, not like my friend
but some acquaintance brushed by on the train.
Had his good fortune kept me from the same,
I had to wonder, a zero sum game
           that gave the night its early end?

Nothing strange. Our drinks were done, that's all.
We haven't spoken since. By morning, I
couldn't remember half of what the guy
had said, just his good news, my slurred goodbye,
                    the click of the latch, the quiet hall.

# Azores

*And me,*
*the temple wall with its votive tablet*
*shows I have offered my drowned cloak*
*to the god of the ocean.*
　　　　　— Horace, *Odes* I.5

*i.*

Heeled over on the sea's domed emptiness,
a sail on the horizon slowly yields
its full size, appearing as a shadow, less
a substance than a rumor blown though fields
that the prevailing wind has furrowed white
and black. Now here it is, an hour on.
The sloop has metamorphosed from a kite
drawn on an unseen string, a distant song
the breeze broke up and scattered in our wake,
to a towering spar beneath a charcoal sky,
gaining, massive, on our tiny stern:
an elephant, a senseless lob of strakes,
whose slow approach we patiently discern,
an unintended sharer lying by.

*ii.*

When the last morning lights fade finally —
each foreign sun run roughshod by our own,
which, hoisted up toward noon, looms large, a stone
scattering sparks along a flinty sea —
I am anxious to have them back again,
crowded above the masthead in light wind,

the pole star amber as we crane to find
true north on nights that show no sign of rain.
The memory of them fades in brightened skies,
a secret so refined it cannot brook
the drab unsubtle breeze and public looks
of post meridiem, the way your eyes
spoke candidly to me at first and then
admitted nothing when I looked again.


*iii.*

The vision of a sunset on the ocean:
countless tongues of flame, as if a wood
had roared up just as evening set in motion
its day's-end rituals of neighborhood.
Nearby shelters shudder in the smoke.
In the middle of this fire, there is no reason,
only a vague account of something broken
that we will not miss now — not in this season
of ember-glow and godsent conflagration.
It will be hours on, when the lost light
cools the scene back to sense, that the relation
of what was to what remains will tinge the night
with an acrid fog still clinging in the air
like a manifest of what's no longer there.


*iv.*

If there is one sustaining fact, it's this:
horizon — Manichean anchor of
our darkening half-world, binding the grays above
the main with breaking waves and constant hiss.

Consider for a moment that the line
you gaze along is not the sea and sky,
but sliding forms, a drama for the eye,
a plum disturbance, cello chords, a seine
of drenched debris clogging the world below.

Aloft: a gauzelike exhale and a haze
through which a searchlight sears its blooded rays.
These masses point to nothing we can know.
Perhaps, just this: that it's not possible
to pin the spirit by an act of will.


*v.*
Hove to:  the tiller lashed and set against
a backing foresail trimmed to contradict

a strong impulse to fall off from the wind:
two canceling passions, each one meant to end

the other's outsized wish to turn away
and toward:  each countermands the other's sway,

until the bow lies flummoxed in the gale,
stunned and bleating, as the rigging flails

and, heaving, we lie on the cabin floor.
This is what it is to live at war:

sleeplessness, recrimination, shame,
rage, paranoia, cleaving, and the name —

like poison — on my lips no longer the same
one I conjured with before the weather came.


*vi.*
The sky this morning — a scar, whose low sun
                    trails breath-shadows over teak,
like Eros flying past on parchment wings
— turns enemy.
                Our natural state is sickness:
*(But, as in sickness, did I loathe this food).*
What in the weather changes, such that wind,
which needled us to make our way across
now wants us gone,
                    with no trace remaining
of the hull that held us, or the sails
that bellied, as lungs fill, with the very force
of — not love — but aspiration, at least?
Drowned, who could then point to us and say . . .


*vii.*
The eye, at dawn, finds no significance
or object carved into the marble sea
that a pilot could dead reckon from, the lee
as blank as what's to windward. Slow advance,
as stark division swallows its own heels —
the round horizon ends where it begins,
repeatedly, a cyclorama of winds,
a lens trained on high cloud banks that reveals
nothing but blur.
                    Below, the fleshy swells

charge on like herds scenting some distant cue
to move. They crowd together toward a new
safety, harbored and far from warning bells,
till the last rays of the sun recede, then fail,
again without the sighting of a sail.


*viii.*

The sheets and stays go slack in renewed calm,
and, for the first time in a week, our thoughts
race free above this skin of shallow troughs.
Hardly-moving waves caress the helm,
as the same stream that urged us on for days
now presses to our sides a guileless hand,
and trade winds peter, free of flux. We stand
unhitching reefs, transfixed by the small ways
sound reasserts itself without the wind:
the gauzy rush of breath, a wheeze of line,
the halyards' endless ticking finally gone
in a warm repose that sunset can't rescind.
We wash ourselves, removing streaks of brine,
new baptized in an hour of halcyon.


*ix.*

A green island draped in volcanic smoke,
imperceptible at first, until the reek
of musk wafts to us seaward over a league,
like the pong of love-sheets a summer night has soaked,
retaining, in the after-dawn, the very smell
that brought the madness on. All this we know
before the misted hills float into view.

The fact of land's not what your dreams foretell.
Its bitter law, a wafer on the tongue:
we are not suited to live long at sea.
Though shoreward-days run down as certainly,
they are a habit that we can't unlearn,
like lines creasing the smooth palm of the hand,
this lust for water, fidelity to land.

# 333 East 68th Street

On moving day, we mopped the scuffed-out floors,
        amazed at the way the place
had shrunk and how completely dust abhors
a vacuum. Stranded by the doorjamb lay
a tousled broom, a scrap of our old lives.
How had we shoehorned so much of our lives
into four flaking cubes? These rooms had been
our cornucopia and gilded age,
chockablock with babyflesh, a din
that mingled love-cries, clatter, childhood rage.

To see them now, they look so blank, so cheer-
        less that, if it wasn't in
our bones, we'd hardly know we touched ground here,
let alone kept house — first you and then,
when we were married, the two of us, then more:
a skittering dog, a girl, twin boys. With more
bodies than rooms, we made our peace with mess,
close-quartered in chaos, riotously
off-kilter and yet willing to confess
that all our wordless plans had come to be.

Out the bedroom window, through the green
        of the garden, a bell
announces the consecration of the scene
from which we're now outcasts. You say, "Ah, well,
it wouldn't be Eden if we could stay."
But more than anything we wish to stay

and like Masaccio's Adam, I cast a glance
that syncs with yours, until we look away,
then down, and realize it's not just chance
but our forsaking that makes the memory.

Who bothers to look for what's not lost?
        Some morning, on the bus,
we'll pass this very street marbled in frost
and spin around to catch a glimpse of us
crossing with the children to the park.
But it's early, no one's at the park,
the trees are bare, no couple's walking there.
Craning back we'll see the building fade
like gray exhaust resolving into air
and understand the error that we've made.

My own slipup (the one I made alone)
        was that I came to feel
that happiness had worked into this stone,
into the very brickwork ribbed with steel —
the family seat, a locus, a redoubt
against besieging entropies of doubt,
our castle overlooking feudal land.
But my idolatry of worldly stuff
made a nonsense of the goods at hand,
the precious things I had not loved enough.

Emptied rooms make their own affluence.
        What will last longer than
this stately pile, ivy-wreathed and immense?
The memories of a life-befuddled man
or woman who, in recalling her past,

feels her mother's bathrobe swirling past
or her father's kisses, which she'll soon grow out of.
The architecture of intersecting lives
will find a way to stay, like acts of love,
which not in place but perhaps in time survive.

Yet survive *where* we wonder, as the day-
      light slants below the panes.
Not here, of course; beyond that we can't say —
on this coast or another, in refrains
at holidays, in other homes than ours,
where if there is still a remnant that is ours,
there will be no occasion for our knowing it.
Dimness: a few last boxes overflow
with things we've tossed aside or kept in going
and arriving in a new place we call home.

# Acceptance Speech

Accept the things you cannot change:
the bleating clock,
the nightly go
— dog-leash in tow —
around the block,

neural chemistry,
patchy hair,
a longing stare
and x-ray eye,

and the niggling fact
that things will stay
roughly this way,
to be exact.

Forgive the things you cannot have:
the supple bod,
taut undergrads,
a nicer pad,
long chats with God,

an older name,
your peers' respect,
the oll korrect,
unbridled fame,

a sense of ease
in your own skin,
a lighter burden
by degrees.

The life you'd swap for on the train
(sight unseen)
is much like yours
though it appears
more green.

So, why this pain
that shorts the breath
and spoils your health?
You grow serene —

not yet, but after
your will resigns
a few more times
with heavy laughter.

# Tritina for Susannah

The water off these rocks is green and cold.
The sandless coast takes the tide in its mouth,
as a wolf brings down a deer or lifts its child.

I walked this bay before you were my child.
Your fingers stinging brightly in the cold,
I take each one and warm it in my mouth.

Though I've known this shore for years, my mouth
holds no charms of use to you, my child.
You will have to learn the words to ward off cold

and know them cold, child, in your open mouth.

*from* Birds of the Air *(2013)*

# Crane

Paper creased is
with a touch
made less by half,
reduced as much

again by a second
fold — so the wish
to press our designs
can diminish

what we hold.
But by your hand's
careful work,
I understand

how this unleaving
makes of what's before
something finer
and finally more.

# Lazy

I don't say things I don't want to say
or chew the fat with fat cats just because.

With favor-givers who want favors back,
I tend to pass on going for the ask.

I send, instead, a series of regrets,
slip the winding snares that people lay.

The unruffledness I feel as a result,
the lank repose, the psychic field of rye

swayed in wavy air, is my respite
among the shivaree of clanging egos

on the packed commuter train again tonight.
Sapping and demeaning — it takes a lot

to get from bed to work and back to bed.
I barely go an hour before I'm caught

wincing at the way that woman laughs
or he keeps clucking at his magazine.

And my annoyance fills me with annoyance.
It's laziness that lets them seem unreal

— a radio with in-and-out reception
blaring like hell when it finally hits a station.

The song that's on is not the one I'd hoped for,
so I wait distractedly for what comes next.

# Birds of the Air

She's the trunk and they're the blowing branches:
the seagulls mass around her as she scatters
bread crusts grabbed from a plastic grocery bag.
They dip to her, since bread is all that matters.

She casts the crumbs in lamplight, over water,
to gulls who catch her manna on the wing —
snatching their staple needs straight from the air,
the sky replete with every wanted thing,

until it seems that they might live off giving.
Back in the bag, her right hand burrows in
and finds a further hunk of loaf and chucks it
into the glinting sleet. The cries begin,

and, without fail, bread finds another mouth.
After she goes, the dark birds settle back.
They float south with the floes along the bank,
their fortune pitched in wind, the water black.

# Spoils

Money I've made lots of different ways:
back-to-back shifts at the Cumberland Farms,
downing burritos out of the microwave,
late-night entertainment being a wall
of glossy mags behind the register
in racks below the cigarettes and scratchers —
all that honey-colored flesh air-brushed to perfection,
pristine among the milk crates and the soot.
Or: in the gleaming dayrooms of the nursing home,
where I would mop up urine underneath
the wheelchairs of the jittering demented,
who were oblivious, it seemed to me,
to the television they were pointed at.
Lunch hours in the trailer in the lot,
with this sweet misfit kid — my boss — and his
boss, discussing daily what they'd do
if they won the Lottery: retire to Boca.
Buy a Caddy. No, a Lexus.
                              So, one day,
out by the nurses' station, there's these two
patients side-by-side in wheelchairs,
waiting for the nurse to take them back
to their rooms, or maybe down to therapy,
when this old guy, Edward was his name —
Edward, he was famous for this shit.
Edward's sitting there next to this lady,
Ethel, I think her name was. Can't remember.
At any rate, so I'll just call her Ethel

for the purpose of the story, or this part
of it, the point of which I want come to
now, and that is this: Ethel, right?
Ethel's got this great enormous smile
on her face, like Thomas Merton or the Buddha.
It's like her gums stretch from her forehead to her chin,
all molars and gold fillings, and her head
is swaying back and forth in fits, like nodding,
because Edward (you gotta love this guy)
has got his hand way up under her skirt.
And though she only half knows that he's there
she's loving it, just loving it. Old Ethel.
Until the nurses come and separate
the two, and send him packing, full of scolds,
with Edward donkey-laughing, very pleased,
the bad boy of the dayroom and God bless him.
He wasn't the only one;
all the nuts were there: the guy who yelled
"Ay," but long and loud, like *Aaaaayyyyyyyyy.*
*Aaaaaaaayyyyyy. Aaaaaaayyyyyyyyy.*
All day we'd hear him, from the parking lot.
Or the dude with elephantiasis they called Plato,
or the woman turned a hundred who would ask,
"Are you my mother? Are you my mother?"

             And occasionally a bed
would just go empty, overnight, like that.
And one of the regular crew was gone —
to the hospital — and just as often as not
that would be it; they wouldn't come back.
Their photos would come down, the woolen throw
would disappear, the tchotchkes, crosses, slippers,

packed up by a nurse, or family.
Thrown away, mostly. It's amazing how
most of the stuff we live with, cherish, hoard
is so utterly worthless when we're gone,
turned instantly to trash.
                              That's another job
I had. Not regularly, just once or twice.
Clean up after people who had died.
The first time was somewhere out on Long Island.
I was just a year or two out of college,
cold calling for cosmetics companies
in a high-rise on the East Side, six to ten.
So I was glad to get the cash and all the books
I could carry: the guy was a professor,
or a rabbi — Schopenhauer, Aristotle's
*Ethics*. I still have them somewhere here.

But the time I'm really talking about was when
I stole a gold watch from a dying man.
Right?
                His apartment was . . . well, unbelievable.
Peering from the hallway door, it looked
like the inside of a trash compactor.

I was shown in by a man I'd never met.
He knew the man whose place it was: a neighbor.
We'll say this neighbor's name is Mr. V.
His friend was sick, said V., a nursing home.
He wasn't coming back to this apartment,
not dead, you see, but never coming back.
My job was to sort out all of the trash,
which was everywhere, on every surface,

like the very air had sprouted clods of mold,
smelly tumors. Everywhere. More trash.
Clogging up the closets, in the kitchen,
bathroom cabinets, dresser, sofa, sink.
Mostly, it was papers, tiny papers.
He never threw away a single shred.
ATM receipts and old prescriptions —
brown-paper grocery bags stuffed full of them.
And I sat there for hours cramming armloads
of this crap into giant Hefty bags,
big ones, like the ones you use for lawns.
I went through every shoebox, every carton,
sorting every piece before I chucked it.
Why? Because I *had* to sort them all.
Because every now and then I'd find a photo
or a postcard or a letter to this guy,
who had been sick six years, the neighbor said.
So that's why so much stuff: the piles of garbage,
the takeout bags from food he'd had delivered.
Tucked in with all this junk was this guy's life:
Kodaks of him getting off a plane
in the bright Israeli sunshine, with his suit
and dark glasses, his thin tie and the shadow
of his fedora, his smile at being home.
Postcards from someone he loved in Florida.
He ran a successful business, apparently,
jewelry and importing, said Mr. V.
In the closet was a collection of wrist watches,
dozens of them, boxes of old watches,
in every style, for men and women, modern
and antique, both.
                    The one I took was gold,

from the closet where I'd been lying on my belly
for nearly half an hour, excavating
bags of stockpiled clothing. On the floor,
I found these vintage watches with no straps,
and when I knew that old V. wasn't watching,
I stuck two in my pocket. (Two I took,
I remember that now.)
                              As I was leaving,
the neighbor says to me, "You're a good boy.
Take a watch. Go on and pick one out."
I say, "No, I don't usually wear a watch.
No, really, thanks. I really couldn't use one."
The air outside was cold, near Christmastime,
like tonight. And I walked north on Upper Broadway,
to a jewelry store and stopped and bought a band.

What was that, like fifteen years ago?
I've only got the one now.
It doesn't keep good time, and I can't afford
to have it cleaned. I've worn it only once
or twice. To make an impression. So I keep it
in a box inside my closet, and though I haven't
had it out in years I know it's there.
What were they going to do, sell it,
and use the money for the nursing home?
I thought a lot about that, afterwards.
Did he need the money to keep him in that place?
I doubt it, you know. Medicaid, Medicare,
whatever the fuck.
                              It kind of haunts me though,
a little, if you want to know. You know?
I can't ever bring myself to throw it out.

Whenever something bad happens to me,
I think of that watch. Like when you died
so young that way. I know I made it worse —
not being around enough, keeping away
as much as I could till it was too late,
and you'd gone.
                        So, what's the secret of the watch?
A man was dying, and I took his watch.
It was his, and then it wasn't; it was trash.
And now that it is mine, I keep it safe,
until it's time for someone else to clean out
*my* closet, and, whoever's job it is,
he makes off with it or he passes it on
or most likely of all
just drops it into a bag and throws it out.

# Itchy

Hard to reach, so you yank your clothes
getting at it — the button at your neck,
the knotted shoe. You snake your fingers in
until your nails possess the patch of skin
that's eating you. And now you're in the throes
of ecstasy, eyes lolling in your skull,
as if sensing the first time the joy one takes
                in being purely animal.

It's so good to have a scratch,
though isn't it a drag living like this,
jounced on a high wire of impulses,
every wish the same programmed response
to another signal passed from cell to cell,
amounting in the end to a distraction —
if truth be told — from rarer things, thoughts free
                from the anchor-chain of self?

For even the least sweetness, we
behave like the old man on the low wall
I saw outside the hospital today,
who had his hand inside his flannel shirt,
scratching at his chest, trancelike, agog,
his eyelids fluttering like butterflies
in a meadow of snowy Queen Ann's lace.
                I never saw him stop.

Such root satisfaction is like
the dying desert legionnaire's in films,
when he finds, against all odds, a water jug
and, lifting it, delights to feel it heavy.
The score swells, his eyes relume. He yanks
the stopper out, then fills his mouth with sand.
Though, worse: we've seen the film; we know it's sand;
we gulp it anyway.

# Cough

I see you once I've got you down to size,
a two-day-stubble squatter; jail-bait eyes;

the bottle-headed trophy mom; the mentor
always angling his face down from the center

of his universe to shine a light on yours.
The fated anorexic, whose allures

shimmer in the mirror for her eyes
only, denying what her denial denies.

Once you become a cliché I can hate you —
or, treat me tenderly and let me date you.

But that only retards the writing-off
that comes with boredom, amour-propre, or (*cough*)

irreconcilable differences, i.e.,
those things about you that are least like me,

yet just slightly different, my foible's homophone,
so in hating yours I really hate my own.

This keeps the focus where it ought to be —
On whom, you ask? Invariably on. . . . See?

I didn't even have to say it, did I?
I love you so much. No need to reply.

# Free Period

Outside study hall,
it's me, my girlfriend, and a guy
named Rob — bony kid, klutzy
at games, fluent in French.
        He's behind her;

I'm asleep or half-
asleep (it's morning), and, as I
squint into the trapezoid of light
breaking on the bench and me,
        I see him raise

his hand to her head
from the back, so gently
she doesn't notice
him at first, but stands there,
        carved in ebony

and beaten gold:
Stacey's straight black hair
falling in shafts of sun.
He smoothes it down,
        firmly now,

so that she turns,
kind of freaked, as if to say,
"Can you believe it?"
to me still coming to.
        Yes, I guess I can,

I think to myself,
with only a twinge
of jealousy, with admiration,
actually. And pity — since he'd seen
        beauty raw,

        for which humiliation
was the smallest price,
and, dazzled, grasped at it,
not getting hold.
        It wasn't his, god knows,

        or mine, as I,
months later, learned
hopelessly — almost fatally,
it felt — or even hers, though it was
        of her and around her,

        in that freeze-frame
of low sunshine,
with us irremediably young
and strung-out from love
        and lack of love.

# Flatirons

*for Charles Doersch*

i.
From the false summit, coxcomb-cum-arête,
cool thermals underscore our frailties,
past edges where our wingless feet are set
and the long look down dilutes the evergreens.
As sandstone ends, the world of ghosts begins —
they sometimes rise up still in dreams, my love.
With one hand firm, I step onto the skin
of the abyss, embracing what's above
and severing spent ties to the scree below.
The filtered light turns lichen eerie green,
ushering in a world we hardly know,
at least not one we're sure we've ever seen
just so, each climber brand new in his skin,
no longer mired in waiting to begin.


*ii.*
The whisper clings beside you as you rise
along the ice melt, following the chalk.
Its cadence is the thrum behind your eyes;
your trembling, the music of its talk.
No longer trust your arms; they're paid with fear.
Along the rock, the grip that's hidden there,
invisible but sure, will not appear
until you trade your fast-hold for the air,
and, as you reach, it ripples like a pool
in which your newfound safety now reflects:

the diastole of breath becomes the rule
for governing what atmosphere elects —
to claim this height as owed to us in spirit,
although we risk ourselves to answer it.


*iii.*

Free solo: dearest, I am losing you,
not now (one hopes!) but slowly, over time.
Admit that there is nothing left to do
but re-devote our efforts to the climb,
remembering that the second side is less
than a reprieve — more sheer and far from kind —
before the gentle, sloping wilderness
enwraps us and we let go of the sky.
Your living hand guides home my dangled foot.
At gravity's unlikely slant, we smear
across the arkose, knowing that the root
has taken hold deep in the layers. Here,
a thrust-fault pushed up rock, and, as it rose,
it found its altitude in its repose.


*iv.*

Pinned to the face, you close the aperture —
no way looks right, and there is no way down
but keeping on — returning's hot allure
hissing its hollow promises, the sound
of the last support-beam loudly giving way.
What is it that wipes the rock free of direction?
The crystal ceiling that began the day
goes black, almost it seems without detection.

The open door blows shut; the empty glass
brims over and, when raised, is dry again:
time's bait-and-switch. An hour from the pass,
wind drags high clouds across the peak; just then
the air grows cold. Our backs turn to the weather,
as a way comes clear, ascending with no tether.


*v.*

It's when we're most engaged with other things
that the angel enters, a twist in temperature,
a lightness in the chest that we call wings.
Giddy with sacrament and the impure
gluttony of blood and air and skin,
we look with panoramic eyes to where
the earth curls under and the sky begins,
though we ourselves are of this light-shot air,
senses extending without obstacle,
reaching past by rooting down though rock —
obdurate kindness, heaven's window sill.
We are as useless as an open lock,
more insubstantial than a drinking song,
and marked by sandstone long after we're gone.

# Dirty Dan

*for Tom Disch*

I can't remember what the night was like.
It was, *phssh*, twenty- . . . seven? years ago,
before I even knew you. I was home,
from college maybe, hanging out with friends?
Christmas break, it must have been. And cold.
Too bad you never saw him. Too late now,
not just because there's no way Dirty Dan
is still alive (he was ancient, even then),
but more because you are not, so prematurely . . .

So: Dan. I only saw him once. Just once.
I guess that's part of it. It snowed that night.
(Let's pretend that we're both sitting around
in your living room, just telling stories.)
Now, it's my turn, right? So — Dirty Dan.
I swear to god this guy was unbelievable:
this wiry geezer, bug eyed, in a toque,
white short-sleeve chef shirt and a stubble beard.
But wait, hold on, back up. So, this is Dan:
a short-order cook with ice blue, staring eyes . . .
I need to tell you a bit about before.
At any rate, it's late one night, and I'm
home from school on break. I'm seeing friends
and drunk and underage and talking "art"
with Julie and her boyfriend Mitch, who's just
like a miniature professor with bad skin.
He's smart and tweedy and totally insane,
and also so completely full of shit,

which I like. And mostly he likes books,
and getting stoned and talking late. Talk, talk.
And then, long-suffering Julie, small and preppy,
and really very cute, I think sometimes.

One minute, Mitch is spouting Joyce — about
how all he actually wanted was to write
a really good read crammed with lots of jokes
for all his friends to savor, to make them laugh.
Next: the neon blur and flat pink light
of a diner by the park.
                              I remember this:
the snow and cold and Mitch rubbing his hands
together, as he says, "Let's go see Dan,"
then we're in a booth.
                              The place is packed.
It's 3 a.m., and there must be a dozen
booths like ours. The counter's jammed with kids
who've come from Luna, dancing, high and freeze-framed
in strobe flashes and ethereal black light.
And now they're beat and hungry, after-hours,
giving up their orders to these guys,
also kids, who write down all the coffee
and toast and juice and ham and bacon sides,
the eggs — fried, scrambled, over easy, up —
and call them out across the room to Dan.
Our voices mingle in the greasy air,
talking bullshit, screaming with delight,
goofing, over which the waiters' voices
fly like homing birds,
                              while, at the grill,

Dan shuttles like a Chinese acrobat,
balancing every order in his mind
like so many plates spun on wooden dowels,
never dropping one, and grunting out
he'd got the order, pick up twenty-one.
And we were there to watch. And snarl-haired Mitch,
who, I just remembered, lost a tooth,
or, no, he had a denture he'd remove
that left this gaping hole each time he'd laugh.
We laughed all night that night.
                              That's why we got
together in the first place, why we drank
and smoked and talked of books. That's why we went
to see Dan in his kitchen, to be amazed,
the way that the whole diner was amazed,
the way the kids who took the orders were amazed.
Dirty Dan was this incredible
freaking genius. Brilliant. You think it's easy?
Try it. What he did was just not something
anyone can do; he knew it, too.
You could tell. How he would yell in a rage
when two of the kid waiters talked at once,
screwing up his groove — and they'd apologize,
since the last thing they wanted to do was break
his perfect streak that ran till 5 a.m.
It was like riding down the trough of a wave
that started somewhere out in the Pacific.
God, how we roared. That's all we really wanted
was to laugh.
                    And you were like that, too, I guess.
That's the way it always went, wasn't it?

Open the wine, talk books, reel off new jokes
that always had some place inside the flow
of a larger conversation for the night,
and a place, too, in breaking the tick, tick,
of dingy sink, cold coffee, quiet phone,
afternoon nap, and too much television,
which haunted you in daylight till the night
came back and, ranting, after-hours, we'd people
the vastness with our stories and we'd laugh.

Now you're dead, I wonder more and more
whom I should tell them to, stories like this,
running through them in my head mostly.
Julie and Mitch? *Pfft.* I can't really say
what happened to them. Did they ever marry?
I doubt it.
Julie must have had more sense than that.
Don't get me wrong; Mitch was my friend, too.
(He was the one who called him Dirty Dan,
cackling and growling with his gap-tooth grin.)
We were a lot alike.
Now I don't know where they are. Alive?
Somewhere? Nowhere?
                        Too long ago to know. I laugh
a lot less with them gone. Does that surprise you?

# Minding Rites

This guy I know, a rabbi, Friday nights,
on his way home before sunset in winter,
always stops at a florist or bodega
and buys a bunch of flowers for his wife.

Every week the same, a ritual,
regardless of her mood that morning, fresh
upsets at work, or snarling on the bridge;
he brings her roses wrapped in cellophane.

But isn't there a ring of hokiness
in that? Why should a good man have to show
his devotion? Some things go unspoken;
some things get tested on the real world,

and isn't that the place that matters most?
So when you told me I should bring you flowers,
I joked, "But don't I show my feelings more
in dog-walks, diapers, and rewiring lamps?"

The flowers, I learned later, weren't for wooing,
not for affection in long marriage, but
for something seeded even deeper down,
through frost heaves, and which might be, roughly, peace.

(It's funny that I just assumed romance.)
Now there's no peace with us, I wonder what
they might have meant to you, those simple tokens,
holding in sight what no rite can grow back.

# Tomorrow & Tomorrow

*A travesty*

I.

"What's done cannot be undone."

Am I right?

So . . . obvious. So irrefutable.
*Of course*, if it is done it can't be undone.
Any idiot knows that. Or else:
"If it were done, when 'tis done, then 'twere well
it were done quickly."

"When the hurly-burly's done."

"Is execution done on Cawdor?"
"Yet let that be
Which the eye fears, when it is done, to see."
You see? Stuff happens, you can't take it back.
Just one of those things you don't have to say,
but sometimes we still need reminding of:
"What's done is done." So good, it's like a spell,
a charm, a bell: *done, done.* But Lady Macbeth?
She wasn't the only one who said it; no,
others said it. Sophocles, for instance,
he said it, something like it; said it long
before her, if you want to know the truth.
Lots of people said it, and it's true.

I did that play, a million years ago.
And every night I'd listen from the wings
and hear those lines.

I was an actor. Sort of.

Or, technically, more like a waiter. So,

I'd pick up part-time shifts behind the bar,
serving Mai Tais underneath the whale
at the American Museum of Natural History —
revolving-door jobs in the service industry
broken up by brief forays on stage.
Here's a couple more, in case you missed it:
"In every point twice done and then done double."
"I have done no harm."

                      (That's what they always say.)


The show was a disaster. Every night,
we died a dozen deaths on different stages.
Macbeth and Lady, they were really married,
married in real life, and they produced it.
In Germany — in English but in Germany.
In western Germany before the wall
came down.
            The other waiters were so excited
when they heard I got a job, that I was Malcolm,
they bought me drinks and gave me this old book:
a beat-up phrase book unearthed at the Strand,
Berlitz or something, and completely worthless.
It must have been from fifty years ago.
Oh, and it had lots of useful stuff,
like "Es tut mir leid, ich brach meine Platte,"
which means, I think, "I'm sorry, I broke my plate,"
or other things I probably would need
like "Ist es Zeit für meine Spritze?":
"Is it time for my injection?"
I remember looking over at my girlfriend
just then — Sasha, a dancer. That made her laugh.
Her teeth were too big and a bit off-center

in a way that made me always want to kiss her.
              "I go, and it is done;
the bell invites me."

        Before we left, we froze our asses off:
rehearsing in some empty public school
on 6<sup>th</sup> and B — no heat and no hot water,
when people slept in tents in Tompkins Square.
Kids would throw M-80s off the roofs —
these huge explosions — and we'd have to run for it.
We'd step outside to smoke a cigarette,
and they'd come streaming down like, *holy shit!*
By dark, the place cleared out:
syringes in the walkups, random gun-pops,
vials strewn in doorways like bright glass
from a car wreck.
              So, I told my waiting job
so long and stuffed a backpack full of clothes.
I can't remember what we said that morning,
Sasha and I. There's lots I don't remember.
Though some of it's still there, a skin, invisible.
Some things you never quite recover from.
I left. So what was I supposed to do?

              You know the curse?
You're not supposed to say the word *Macbeth*;
instead you say the "Scottish Tragedy,"
which sounds ridiculous, but there you have it.
Let's say we're talking in the dressing room,
and I say the name Macbeth, you know, accidentally.
Actors have this thing, they have this code
(or not a code; it's more of a behavior):

I'm supposed go outside and close the door.
I turn around three times, say *shit* or *fuck!*
and then I knock and ask to come back in.
It's kind of cool, 'cause then it's like a safety,
like canceling something bad: you take it back.
But cursed? Do people ever think they are?
Who thinks they're cursed? You think, well that's not good,
or that's a string of bad luck, a bad year,
but no one thinks they're cursed. Not at the time.

The play was bad, no doubt.
                              It wasn't that.
Some things just sort of happened. Little things
at first, annoying stuff, like props gone missing.
But then we crashed the van: Lady Macbeth
was driving. She spun out on the Autobahn
and had to do the tour in a cast —
"Out damned spot . . ." She'd start rubbing the plaster,
night after night, sleepwalking, in a trance.
And after that I did begin to think
that maybe we were cursed. It felt like that,
like we'd done something wrong.
                              It tells you things
that you don't want to know — about yourself,
about how you think that everything is fine,
then one cold morning with the snow outside
you wake up sweating from an awful dream,
convinced that you have done things so unspeakable . . .
What if you did, only you didn't know it?
Or, more likely, knew it, and forgot.
Something you'd never believe in a thousand years:
murder your father, sleep with your own mother,

those kind of things.
But that's a different play.


II.
This is the way the line's supposed to go.
The battle's over, right? We won: our side.
And Banquo spends the night in Macbeth's castle.
He gets there and looks up and sees this swift
nesting among the rafters there. This scarred
old warrior, this patriarch of kings
is so moved by the sight of this, he makes
a joke about the song birds having sex.
He sniffs the air and says:
                              *This guest of summer,*
*The temple-haunting martlet, does approve,*
*By his loved mansionry, that the heaven's breath*
*Smells wooingly here; no jutty, frieze,*
*Buttress, nor coign of vantage, but this bird*
*Hath made his pendent bed and procreant cradle.*
*Where they most breed and haunt, I have observ'd*
*The air is delicate.*
                    Something like that.
So, our guy comes.
                    Our Banquo's name is Bill,
and Bill's this graying hippy from the Village,
who pays a dollar-fifty rent, he says,
which frees him up to do a bit of acting.
So, Bill comes out; he looks up in the grid,
with three or four of us just standing there,
and Duncan, who's the king, so hugely fat
he's like a minivan. So, Bill looks up.

(He's downstage.) He looks down. He looks at us:
"This . . . bird," he says.
                         And he's completely up:
that's when you're off the script, you're up, you're *up*.
You've no idea who you are or what
you're doing.
                    It's, I guess, a bit like drowning,
like being under water, but too deep.
You go into a kind of panic mode —
the world slows down and hangs there at a distance.
From the cold murky bottom you look up
and see the small disk of the sun receding,
and you realize you haven't got the air
to get back up. So you begin to swim,
then lose your bearings in a cloud of bubbles.
King Duncan sees this — Duncan's name is Neil —
Duncan sees that Bill's completely jammed,
so what he does is . . . throw the guy a bone?
Skip ahead and pick up later on?
No, no. He stands there, doesn't say a word,
steps forward even, sort of cranes his neck,
as if to say, "Uh-huh? We're list-en-ing."
I tell you, actors — they're a pack of dogs,
completely warped.
                         Still, it was all good fun.
Lady's in a cast, the show's a bomb.
Not even knowing German, we could tell
the papers thought we were a total joke.
But we were getting paid and seeing sights
and drinking beer. A lot.

I can't forget that show, and not because

I was freest then or wildest or whatever;
just, parts of it keep coming back that way.
Or, earlier:

           It's snowing. We're on Jane Street,
with wood smoke rising from the townhouses.
Sasha's in lace-up boots and woolen tights,
short skirt from which her dancer's legs
are shooshing in the cold.
She's pouting over something, and I'm hanging
on every word and sigh, on every turn
of her moods, and there were many, same as me.
Across the avenue, up sagging steps
to a tiny place she shared with another girl.
The roommate hated me, 'cause every night
we'd show up late then quickly disappear
into the bedroom — closet, crawl space, lair,
barely big enough to squeeze a mattress in —
and close the door and make love with the lights on.
I would call her name out like a chant,
repeating it with every exhalation,
soft in her ear at first, then loud, then louder,
as we fell backward over a high wall
into blankness.
           It's stuff like that stays with you.
So, when her voice came to me over the line
in a phone booth in Cologne, near the cathedral,
the gist of it was like the crack of ice
constricting on a mountainside, and I
realized if I hung up the phone
that would be it.

There's someone outside waiting for the booth.

After five minutes in the ice and snow,
he starts banging on the door as if to say
when will you be done, I need the phone.
And I'm behind the glass, just hanging on,
and asking her how come she's back with him.
*He's in the room. I think I almost hear him.*
I know because she used to talk to him that way.
He'd call when I was there, and she'd pretend
I wasn't, which was cruel of her and sexy.
He's right there, and she's naked, on the edge
of the futon and it's nine o'clock in the morning.
And now the German guy starts hammering
his fist against the booth, so I just stop.

It's funny: I remember bits and pieces:
the caramel-colored duvet and the curl
her lip made when she smiled, her body leaning
above me, choking laughter hoarse with tears,
the way her eyes were like a little kid's.
I thought, that's it, you know?
                                                    I started reading
the Bible. I tore out the Old Testament
and carried it around. But you don't die.
You live for longer than you think you will.
Of course, there's things that won't let you forget
how what you wanted is what hurt you most,
how it was happiness itself betrayed you.

"Well, let's away and say how much is done."

III.
Snow was piling up knee-deep in Munich,
at least where we were staying in the cramped
side streets near the station — a Turkish slum.
And we were in a war.

                    "Kein Blut für Öl"
was scrawled in red spray paint across the walls.
They didn't want us there. Nobody did.


                    "We are all Germans here,"
some radish-faced Bayerische drunkard yells
over the Beatles in the Café Americain —
that's right, the goddamned Café *Americain*.
He yells it at Macduff, an Irish guy,
(not Scots, but close enough for bus and truck).
We got a lot of that, both north and south.
So, here's the Black Forest. Here's the North Sea.
Let's say this squiggly line's the Autobahn,
and every day we'd drive at record speed
from Aachen to Stuttgart, Stuttgart to Freiberg,
Freiberg to Cologne, four towns a week.

Because I'm Malcolm, I get to be the king,
which I thought was pretty cool, except, get this,
my grand finale always got a laugh.
I'm up there heaving out my guts, and just
as I start to raise the crown above my head
with stage light pouring through this golden O
(a moment that you dream about in school)
  — that's when the laughter starts.
                              And not just giggles.
No, no. A nervous laugh, like wildfire.

It wasn't my acting, though that was bad
enough — more lame than laughable, I'm sure.
They laughed because each night, right at the curtain,
they'd fly in a giant banner of my head
to replace the one they'd torn down of Macbeth.
The drops were painted by some kid in Queens,
with tempera paint or house paint, I don't know.
So, when they dropped the thing, each night we'd hear
this far-off rumble like an engine grinding.
This floor-to-ceiling banner of my face
was fucking cross eyed. You believe that shit?

Did you ever see Polanski's film of *Macbeth*?
It's got great stuff. But mostly that's because
Kenneth Tynan told him what was what.
That Banquo's children shall be kings, we know.
We also know that Malcolm's on the throne.
So, here's the thing.
Macbeth has got no kids, none that we know of.
But Lady's given suck, that's how she puts it,
so what is that? What happened to her kid?
(I know, I'm getting literal.) Behind the credits,
a figure in a cloak — who must be Banquo's son —
goes to see the witches. It never ends.
One thane betrays another, blood for blood,
blood against blood. And so on and on.
Sometimes it's hard to know how it began,
how what they wanted was the thing they wanted.
"What's to be done?"
                              Days off we used for sightseeing:
end of the streetcar line, there is the fence,
then squares marking the places that they slept.

Behind is the iron door that kept the flames,
and overhead the sky where they saw the smoke.

The gate on which we read the words was here.
Behind the gate, the path bends to the left.
The crematorium is sort of here.

Half of us could easily have died there.
Half of us would have been the ones who lived.


IV.
I don't want to talk about it. Only . . .
change the subject, can we? Twenty years,
so long I can't remember who I was.
Though mostly I'm the same. I have the same
marks set down against me on the slate.
That's how I think of it sometimes, like marks,
like hatch marks on a perfect field of white.

*The sun is setting in you, the snow is falling in you . . .*

I hate this song. It's crap.
                              And mostly I
Don't think about it, really. Why do that?
I only get more miserable that way.
We'd talk at night. He'd call from Germany.
He was in a play. So, yeah, we'd talk.
Which was the worst, since months went by
that I couldn't tell him. I just couldn't.

*Your face is like a mirror, your face inside my mirror . . .*

I prayed, you know, that it might not be true:
the lateness. Then I'm ten or twelve weeks on,
and he's off god-knows-where, calling me up
on Sunday mornings. I think I kind of lost it.
Enough, I thought, enough, you know? I told him
I was back with my old boyfriend. That was it.
He never called me after that. Which scared me.

*How can it be the same, if it was never that way?*

It was just simpler on my own, and I
didn't want to know what he would say . . .
didn't want to hear him make that sound
like I should know exactly what to do.
I had no help, and I did what I did,
the only thing that at the time made sense.
A life ago. That's not me anymore.

*It's just the tide of your eyes, washing away the shore.*

You can hear church bells from here. If you
wait a minute we can hear them now.
The bells are like the snow. They make things quiet.
And when they ring then everything around them
is quiet and the sound of quiet is
the sound between the rings, between the noise.
The same with snow, especially when it's new.

I love the snow, the way it wipes the street
clear for a little while, before the dogs,
before the plows make muddy hills of it,
before the road-salt and the sidewalk-salt

dissolves it into dirty lakes and streams.
For a second it is clean and blank and quiet.
It's a miracle, how muted it can be,

like all the sound's absorbed into itself.
I like to stand outside there, on the street,
without the traffic in the early morning
with a new snowfall blanketing the street,
only my breath like feathers in the cold.
That's when I talk to God — don't laugh at me —
and actually feel for sure he's listening.

This one time I was driving, New Year's Day.
I was driving to a friend's. The road was empty.
It was early, just me and the snow
on long slow curves between two mountain peaks:
a whiteout — road and trees and sky all white,
snow falling like a bed sheet on the hood.
Then, around a bend, a shadow in the road.

I didn't slow down. It was just a shadow.
But then, too late, I saw it was a deer
that had been run down by another car.
I wound up skidding halfway off the road.
When I got out, the place was a cathedral
with giant walls of white, even the deer
seemed pristine, a perfect antlered buck,

except for the halo of frozen blood
around its head. Its eyes were filled with snow,
I felt sick, kind of queasy, and I thought
that I should do something for this deer

like drag him to the shoulder, but I just
left him in that paradise of snow.
Was it the blood that made it seem so holy?

You bleed when you get a tattoo, don't you?
Sometimes I think of getting one. Today,
I woke up after dreaming that I had one,
in brilliant colors on a white background,
a streak of purple written into white,
on the slope of my back, all across my back,
indelible against a field of white.


V.
I met this girl in Freiberg after the run,
where someone had a car, and we piled in
for the Schwartzwald hairpin drive to Prague for Easter.
The fields were filled with Soviet concrete,
with rusted pylons and abandoned trains,
just drying out like carrion in the sun.
In one small town, I crapped into a hole
in the ground from which a board had been removed.
We stayed a couple days in a family flat
belonging to some Czech friends of the girl —
Greta? — who later let me in her sleeping bag.

But it was after, in her dorm, the others gone,
when we actually shared a bed. By now it's spring.
On the morning of the day that I was leaving,
we made love in the cold lattice of sunlight
that came in through her window. It was nice,
and I remember thinking that my girlfriend

could care less who I slept with. I was happy
that I had someone, that soon I'd be leaving.
I felt giddy. I felt wrung out and loved,
if only briefly. Though it wasn't love
I felt exactly — more like free of love.
I was glad when it was time to get away,
to Paris on the night-line sleeper train.

An oubliette — a train inside a tunnel.

"Was not that nobly done?"

I saw her one more time back in New York —
Sasha — and then again, I guess about a year ago,
six or seven months before she died.
It was a suicide. I should have told you that.
She seemed okay, you know? She seemed . . . the same.
We drank a fifth of Scotch out of the bottle.
I was so wasted out on Amsterdam,
feeling sick and walking toward the train,
with the cold coming on and early dusk.
Seems a long time ago.
"I gin to be aweary of the sun . . ."

Sunlight shone on her face inside the diner:
Is the body ever holy except in memory?

I learned
that I was capable of anything.

# A Stop before Starting

The only time I've been to Switzerland
was early one spring on a train through the mountains.
There was a lake — I guess it was Lucerne?
Above me cliff-tops ridged with snow fanned out
so that where I stood at the edge of the platform
light bathed the empty siding all around
with a diffused opalescence off the water.

Behind the station must have been a town,
spires of churches, municipal arcades,
and coffee squelching in the fogged cafés.
I never saw the place, though I remember
thinking *this* is Switzerland and took
a mind-shot of the pines, breathing-in the cold
as the porter whistled at us to reboard.

# The Landing

Light goes pink on
the hulls of working boats
and on the boulders cropping out
from green islands opposite.
What's pent and riled

slackens, as ripples
lead our eyes along the passage.
The most difficult part is over,
the hardest is now past.
Twin vapor trails

crisscross under
Scorpio. When a horse
shakes off its traces, it begins
to forget the lash, takes
shade and pungent hay.

What a fine day
it has become. From
the landing, I see the breeze
feathering the inlet. Such
excellent timing.

And you have come
too, as I thought you might,
wordless at the water's edge.
And whether or not we
wind up like this

in time — as likely
it will be some antiseptic bed
or hairpin turn banded by ice —
my hope is this: just then,
I'll meet you here.

*from* Black Sea *(2018)*

# Night Blind

There's a spot
at the top
of the street,
where the lamp

is out, that's
the darkest
part of the
block. I don't

go that way
at night, though
it would be
all right,

I know. No one's
there, just
a chained-up dog
in damp air

and branches
too dark to see,
like black water
churning.

# Living Room

God sees me. I see you. You're just like me.
    This is the cul-de-sac I've longed to live on.
Pure-white and dormered houses sit handsomely

along the slate-roofed, yew-lined neighborhood.
    Past there is where my daughters walk to school,
across the common rounded by a wood.

And in my great room, a modest TV
    informs me how the earth is grown so small,
ringed by spice routes of connectivity.

My father lived and died in his same chair
    and kept it to one beer. There's good in that.
Who could look down upon, or even dare

to question, what he managed out of life?
    Age makes us foolish. Still, he had a house,
a patch of grass and room to breathe, a wife.

It's my house now, and I do as I please.
    I bless his name. I edge the yard, plant greens.
Our girls swing on the porch in a coming breeze.

# Café Future

The bunting they put out for the grand opening
never got put away, so every day

looks as if it might be opening day.
You inquire if Café Future carries pie,

and sure enough it's right there on the menu.
A slice of rhubarb and black coffee, please.

The pie tastes like you'd hoped it would, but sweeter.
And though you're wary of newfangledness,

you've never had a piece of pie this good.
You think you'll make the Future your new place.

The long counter's reflected in plate glass,
where sunlight pours in from the parking lot,

and the guy who's looking back at you is you
and not quite you. The morning rush is over.

The chrome gleams with a perfect gleaminess.
The waitress's smile lets you know she agrees.

It makes you want to stay and eat more pie.
She comes by, young looking, like her own daughter,

and whisks your plate away. Another slice.
I know I really shouldn't. Just one more.

That's fine with her, she says. She's on a double
and happy to bring you pie all day long.

# The Chain

Outside Giant,
a woman, whose child —
one of three, all under ten,
and this one maybe five,
a girl — is going wild,
crying (keening really),
up the canned-goods aisle,
past the Wonder,
crazed, noncompliant,
face borscht red,

now breaks down
herself — the mom, I mean —
grabbing the kid by the coat.
She pulls her close and screams
something PG-13
in the half-full parking lot,
not caring that we've seen
her lose her shit.
Two cars down,
a guy, foot-lit

by tail lights,
starts tsking as he pops his trunk,
saying good and loud, for me to hear,
"That's no way to treat your kid."
He wobbles like he's drunk
or has bad hips, slides

into his piece of junk
and turns it over.
His brights
illuminate the river

of rain
bubbling like sea spray
across the pocked anchorage
in which our cars are moored.
On my way
home, it's still needling me:
What's that guy's deal? Okay,
he has no children. But who's
more insane?
He's sure it's her; I choose

him. And me?
Tonight my son
actually flinches as he turns
the corner, still stinging from my swat,
with his Nerf gun
cocked. He paints the enemy,
remembering him red-faced, gone
ballistic, flashing teeth.
Down his sights, he
squints and aims at me.

And I agree:
they will be in his mind
forever, the image of me raging
and the look on his mother's face.
Will he, in his turn, find

a different way to be? So far,
he is, in his finer moments, kind.
       Other times he'll turn
            raw, like me, and like me
      will not learn.

# New Town

The storm-light and the blowing bales of leaves,
mountainous clouds, the frequent gusts of rain,
humidity that makes him sweat at night:
this wasn't the way it was in the old town.

In homeroom he has to stand without a desk
until a teacher sends him to his place.
When she says his name, thirty faces turn,
and when they look away they don't look back.

His father's still living in the other place.
His mother has appointments during the day.
When he gets home he microwaves a plate
and empties a can for the cat. They eat.

In the dark, his mother, home by eight, can see
the TV beaming through the picture window,
as he paces through a dungeon with a rifle
and fires in an indiscriminate spray

at anything that moves. His mother lies
down with her clothes still on. Soon, she will sleep.
The porch light shows bare trees above the yard
and the rusty sumac in a low-slung sky.

# Weeds

My emerald legions, how tall you have grown:
so many. With what supernatural speed

you overlord the weakest in the garden —
frizzled hydrangeas, sere mint, sun-starved basil.

Tousle-headed, you can see the sky
above the cowering, defeated plots.

This is your day of triumph: eager sugars
rise up through your ramifying stalks.

And I allowed it. My cool inattention
found good reasons to look the other way,

since all that grows is good, or so I thought.
*How soon would height recall high thoughts*, and yet,

if I uproot you now, how I would miss you.
Sweet knotgrass, heartsick briar, purple thistle.

Even tilled up, the garden wouldn't look
as it did when my grandmother warned me

not to grow too fast. She lived to be
a hundred, girlhood lost except for this:

a vague lightness coming, as though of wings
lifting her above the loamy soil,

and all she thought of, as the wind upheld her,
was the packed ground, how tenuous her flight.

Or I imagine so. Though half her age,
I, too, can't quite remember what it felt like

to be light-footed, open to the sun,
without the clogging stems elbowing out

what I meant when I first planted here:
larkspur, geraniums, cilantro, lime.

# Dying the Day Prince Died

                    is the opposite of being born
on the same day as, say, Marie Curie or Bach
or even Prince, for that matter, or the artist
formerly known as The Artist Formerly Known
As Prince. Now, just Prince, as he will
forever be known. Too bad I never met him.
You, I met. A few times, as a matter of fact,
but you never remembered my ever meeting you.
Memory's a tricky thing, and so I forgive you.
Who am *I*, after all? Just a person, with a pulse.
A pulse is good, particularly from your perspective,
I'd imagine. The internet is burning up with the news
of Prince's death, almost literally on fire
with the heat generated by his solo on the all-star
"While My Guitar Gently Weeps" at the Rock and Roll
Hall of Fame. At the end, instead of a mic drop,
Prince throws his guitar up in the air, and as far as
we're concerned, watching it on YouTube,
it never comes down, a guitar-chariot of flame,
its stained-ash body somewhere becoming spirit.

I'm not sure where you died or how exactly.
I heard of it though friends. You had been ill.
There hasn't been a whole lot in the press.
It's possible that I missed it, that we missed it.
We've all been so distracted by the passing
of Prince, by our wish to be purified again
in the waters of Lake Minnetonka, by the terror
of a father's drunken rage, by laughter and the rhythmic
click of boots walking in lamp-lit rain.

# The Consolations

In this abandoned house I got to love
telenovelas. Marta slaps the air
a foot from the face of her once-true love.
Jorge's head jerks back from the force of love,
and, in the storm between them, a supercell
rumbles and lows: after the flash of love,
the usual crack, just slightly late. *Amor
Prohibido*, the snowy TV set
warns them — and us. Their fates supremely set,
they drop into the oubliette of love,
head-over-heels, powerless to counteract
lust's common law, which they soulfully enact.

It doesn't matter that it's all an act;
for me, alone with them, it feels like love.
For desperate lovers, there can be no act
more human than to stumblingly react.
I mouth the words as they fly through the air,
"No sé haría sin ti, mi amore." Both act
the parts that backstairs lovers die to act.
I feel their hurt, its charge, in every cell —
a tongue-tip on a 9-volt Duracell.
Their future, plunging down a cataract,
hides in mist, not clear like at the outset,
upended just as everything was set.

Even with the whip-thin glamorous set,
the turnabout, the unforeseeable act,
a single word, can, in a breath, upset
the plan. The Wheel of Fortune has a set
of rules that are decidedly hard to love.
The take-home consolation is a set
of matching steak knives — *Don't adjust your set.*
*You heard that right. (Are we still on the air?)*
My murmured pleas rise up as thin as air,
a hiss emitted by a wiped cassette.
My food is gone. I have some things to sell.
When they are gone and nothing's left to sell,

the cable will get cut and then my cell.
I sit for six hours at the TV set,
my thoughts a whirligig, a carousel,
one thought in hiding, coiled, a sleeper cell.
On the news tonight: an actor's desperate act.
(I knew him, Horacio.) When does a cell
no longer behave as a healthy cell,
dividing itself for the last time? Love
recedes — as Marta knows — till even love
of comfort and daylight drains off cell by cell.
It's like I'm finally coming up for air
but my lungs burn for something more than air.

Black-and-white movies never go off the air,
and QVC has jewels enough to sell.
A rising generation crowds the air-
waves with its lissome smiles bright as Bel Air.
I dial the hotline. *Busy.* So, I set
the phone down, crack a high window for air.

From here, it's hard to calculate the air
that separates the notion from the act.
I don't remember how I'm supposed to act.
I know now that I cannot live on air.
I know that I no longer live for love.
Pero no se puede vivir sin amar.

The phone is quiet. It's a sign of love.
Friends have all turned their faces from the act.
I cannot move or change the course that's set.
I sound the ardor of the cancer cell,
the mouth that, underwater, gulps at air.

# *Tragedy*

That's quite a title that Franz Kline has given
his late-career oil at the BMA.
Those AbEx cats were really serious,
serious drinkers and serious about their art.
Me, I like the title. But look at this thing:
not stygian or glum, knee-deep in blood.
It's all sunny yellows, except for what
is going on there in the center, gray
and brown and black. The eye attends those later.

First, it's lemons and pinks and blues. And orange.
My god, it's like a sunrise, not a place
where bad things happen. And that's exactly right.
Old Franz Kline knew what he was up to. Sure,
atrocities often root down in the dark.
Ditches make room for limed and fetid bodies.
But they are not the sites of tragedy.
It's when there is no stain of evildoing,
ever. Where poppies overgrow the soil.

Imagine, say, King Lear ceding his kingdom
not in some flinty throne room but a field
surrounded by green hills a league from the sea.
He's dozing in late sunlight, as a few
benign and sluggish bees surround his head.
It's warm. His daughters' robes trail over the grass
and billow like jibs in the saltish breeze.
The nattering of Kent and Gloucester wakes him,

and the king remembers he has work to do.
He rises and strides forward to where a map
the size of a large carpet is unrolled
in blinding light. Sun hits Cordelia's hair;
it blazes yellow. No sign of rain clouds,
and gale-force winds seem unimaginable.
All's perfectly tranquil as the old king
begins to speak of love to his loved daughters.

# Plague

Some ancient stories begin with a famine —
Ilium, Egypt, Thebes. The cause is hidden

from the sufferers, at least for the time being,
though slowly they begin to guess at it.

A mother holds her drowned child in her lap.
A man, to remain a man, is shot to death.

Abandoned and hell-bent, they flee in droves.
Many turn to magic for protection.

And those who foresee red tides get ignored.
The sands, where bodies lie unburied, scroll

past us, in glowing outposts of attention.
Or on nearby streets. Staggering, the number.

What does their ruler — wittingly or not —
keep from them of the evil that began it:

inhuman wrath and blinding counter-wrath?
And in the stalled line of mid-morning traffic,

each driver views the sky through charcoal glass
and feels just how he has a right to feel.

# Stalker

There's a decided lack of flowers in The Zone.
Weeds, sure. And mud. There are no lime-tree bowers in The Zone.

There's a feral dog and lots of poisonous water.
There's three Russians traveling literally for hours in The Zone —

two guys and a close-shorn Stalker (not much of a talker,
that one), on the hunt for mystical powers in The Zone,

whatever those might be. One guy's a writer and super ponderous;
the other's an earnest prof. Why are there no whisky sours in The Zone

That might liven things up a bit. As it is,
one guy sits brooding, as another cowers in The Zone,

curled up like a fetal pig, surrounded by the detritus of a lost world:
ruined dachas and smashed-up towers in The Zone.

These guys are really filthy, too, and must reek to high heaven.
Is there a law against taking showers in The Zone?

Now someone's gone and made a video game of the film.
There's guns and monsters that the "meatgrinder" devours in The Zon

And Chernobyl's in the subtitle for pop-toxic effect,
as Andrei's psychic child, gone before me, glowers in The Zone.

# *from* Black Sea

II. White Jasmine

I must sound like I'm speaking in a foreign language.
      But we adapt. Of course.

      It's not so bad, knowing the names of things,
how to get from home to the harbor, bars

      where they serve drinks laced with absinthe.
Wormwood is for forgetting and early summer.

      A high wind sweeps the stones clean. Each flower
flares briefly like the memory of friends then falls,

      acrid and brown and pasted to the walk.

      A tawny fox wanders the perimeter
of the yard edged with shrubs in bloom & eyes

      birds that perch along the fence.
How easily detail is wrung from the rag of the past,

      no enlivening clues, no tender recognitions,
only the faintest tinge, like a dirty sky at evening, whose

      ochre glow hardly knows it was day.

III. False Holly

This waxy
faker
grows everywhere
here, whole

bushes of it,
gem green
trees ranging
overhead

with such
generosity

& élan,
falsehood
flourishing

as if
it were the
most natural,
God-wanted
thing
in the

world.

IV. Patapsco

The water scums up at the edge of the harbor,
evanescing like beer into sawdust.

Behind the black glass of hurtling cars,
the denizens crane forward, tilt their brows,

jaws set, striated muscle at the bone
& in their inner ear a grinding sound.

They're hard as metal. Cold abandonment
has made them *backwater*.

What keeps me up at night is not the fear
that I will never feel that I belong

to them, but that I will.
They have a hollow look,

as if the soul's drained from the body,
but the soul hangs on, hunkered down behind coal eyes.

They hold the road, fly by, not slowing down.
You've missed your turn. You are already lost.

V. The Long Coat

I saw you walking away from me
across the brown bricks in your long, black coat.
You haven't worn that coat in years,
not since we moved here, where it's not the fashion.
But there you were, your blonde hair comme il faut,
a swim in your step so that the fabric jumped —
such a commanding, youthful figure, such
stride & assurance oh, light, act & balance.
The ground rolled in waves and trees clung to their
last leaves, the ones that had them. It was winter.
And I thought I saw you walking away.


IX. Low Ceiling

The clouds have caused delays. Flights are on hold.
Coming in from the county, traffic stalls
behind an accident we cannot see.
We know it's there & know it must be bad.

We are absolutely stuck. It makes me angry,
makes me want to find the one whose fault
this is. God damn it, damn it, *damn*. I'm fine.
Can't remember if I took my Lexapro.

Or maybe it's because I gave up smoking.
I'm investing in my future. It feels good.
But why are all these duplexes abandoned?
*Prejudice* just means our minds are made up

beforehand. It's not that we're afraid of failure;
we long ago foresaw all this would fail.
The sky seems grayer than it's ever been.
Windowless façades open on thin air.

And now we're finally moving past the wreck.
Some van with tinted windows slows enough
to look and know *At least it wasn't me*,
cruising over a shoal of raw green gems.


X. Aubade

I wake up in my old house,
squinting at the seam of light
gilding the flowered curtains,
as six flights down the city's up before me.
Across the street, a woman in green
unchains the gated park. The block
fills with taxis. The light turns,
and turns back without me.

# On the Death
# of a House Plant

My Christmas cactus is dead. Dead. O blameful
house sitter, who cared more for having sex
in my bed with your girlfriend of the hour,
sleeping in and watching Netflix, drinking beer.
Thank you for the briefs you left behind.
I thought I'd wash and wear them as some meager
recompense for the life that you cut short,
but I did not. That plant was hard to kill.
Believe me. When I found it years ago
in the apartment of the girl I later married,
I thought it wouldn't make it. But it struggled
through our dating and our breakup, the engagement —
which, by the way, was wrought by long-stemmed flowers.
It lived through a change of city — twice.
It wouldn't bloom at first and never would,
I thought. But over the years tender new sections,
soft as eyelids, tentatively appeared,
and then, each winter, fuchsia flowers.
Here is the window where it took its light.
The untold thoughts that swirled around my head
like dust motes, as I looked out through the stems
of this familiar friend, I've put away.
It will bloom again in heaven, but never again here.
I blame myself. I was away too long.

# Let

Across the net,
she wilts and falls
behind, so I let
a few balls

slide by
in the midgy air
and drawn sky
of late summer.

Is this
letting her win
a Judas kiss —
the warm sin

of fooling too
far a daughter
who,
slow to laughter,

stakes all in all
on a game?
She's tall.
I call her name,

to snap her
back from the place
she goes, blur-
ring the odds: ace,

game, set.
Her stride returns,
as I abet
her. She learns

no lesson, nor
do I hint
at helping. After,
we sprint

on the road
home, our run
hung with gold
silk spun

by spiders in
patchy pines.
The threads glint
in sidewise lines,

cinches borne
by the air,
so loosely worn
they're hardly there.

# Low Pressure

*for Nick*

He's still too small to fix the sail,
so I help him rig the rolling dinghy.
He wants to go off in the wind,
and before I can unhitch the bow
      he's heading out.
I like watching him scud along.
I suck air when he dips the rail
into the freezing current, jibing
hard or stuck in irons, trying
        to come about.

Keeping in harbor is the rule,
but it's still beyond where I can swim.
I call (too loud) when he's far enough.
*I've got it, Dad*, he hollers back
      into the breeze.
Worry tastes of bile, like rage.
He's learned how to read the wind
but doesn't know what wind can do
without warning and heedlessly.
      He has an ease

that makes my caution cowardly.
I see the bar he dares me with,
the rock that at low tide rides clear,
the seconds that stretch in the eye,
      the wave-washed pier.
What's the point? He can't hear me now.

He's scared of zombies, not of reefs,
his nightmares full of nothing real.
No use in saying the words I think,
*My dear, my dear.*

# Keats in Louisville

His copy of Audubon's *Ornithology*
was worth a million dollars at his death,
to say nothing of his older brother's letters.
John dreamed of the New World but never saw it.
George, on the other hand, made the frontier his,
kept his coin close but paid the consumptive's debts.
Keats the businessman, Keats of Kentucky,
Keats for whom they named Keats Avenue,
a quarter-mile of trees and clapboard houses.
The one Keats brother to outlive his twenties,
he kept three slaves and died at forty-four.

# The Rock Balancer

Dead still, as if breathing with the rock,
he lifts a boulder in his grit-flecked hands
then tilts it to its base of smaller stones,
rotating it minutely back and forth,

until he feels it grab, or leap up, freed
of gravity by keeping faithful to it,
an arabesque on pointe, antic inversion,
a chair poised on an acrobat's raised chin

or climber taking slack above a vale.
Harsh granite makes a harmony with air.
Most days the cairns survey the beach alone,
a stark coast guard outfacing a cold sea,

but today he's with them, kneeling on the sand,
their maker, Ben Gunn–bearded, driftwood boned.
He rents a room near here. By afternoon,
save for the odd seabird, they'll keep their own

mute company, the big-heads, standing out
in a steady drizzle, as across the street
the cafés cover tables in blue tarps
and the tide draws off the shore as they look on.

## The Author

David Yezzi's latest books of poetry are *Birds of the Air* and *Black Sea*. He is the editor of *The Swallow Anthology of New American Poets*, foreword by J. D. McClatchy. His verse play *Schnauzer*, produced by the Baltimore Poets Theater, is available from Exot Books. A former director of the Unterberg Poetry Center of the 92nd Street Y in New York, he teaches in the Writing Seminars at Johns Hopkins.

Printed in the USA
CPSIA information can be obtained
at www.ICGtesting.com
LVHW051613221123
764524LV00032B/997/J